Published by
News International plc
P.O. Box 495
Virginia Street
London E1 9XY

Printed and bound in Great Britain by Caledonian, Glasgow
Designed and typeset by Gordon Beckett, Lee Herneman
and Ian Mooney.

ISBN   1 902254 11 2

The Sunday Times
LONDON

The publisher would like to acknowledge the following photographic copyrights:
p19 © Sutton Images; p23, p91, p119 © Simon Townsley; p29 © André Camara; p35 ©
David Giles; p37, p123 © Stuart Clarke; p 41, p69 © Des Jenson; p45, p141 © Peter
Trievnor; p49 © Justin Sutcliffe; p51, p85, p105, p111, p151 © Francesco Guidicini; p55,
p71, p95, p129, p131, p145 © Jeremy Young; p63 © Denzil McNeelane; p75 © Martin
Beddall; p79 © Steve Etherington; p83, p99 © Bob Collier; p89 John Carlos; p 23, p103,
p109, p135 © Andy Watts; p115 © Ashley Coombes; p 125 © S. Gibson; p139 © Peter
Whyte; p147 © Justin Williams; p153 © Derek Ironside Photography.

Every effort has been made to trace all copyright holders but if any has been inadvertently
overlooked, the publishers will be pleased to make the necessary arrangement.

My First Break

How Entrepreneurs Get Started

42 interviews from the pages of
The Sunday Times

by Rupert Steiner

Dedicated to my brave grandmother

Acknowledgements

I am grateful to all the entrepreneurs for their encouragement and patience and agreeing to give up so much of their time to be interviewed. Thanks also to Tobias Steed, Juliette Bright, and Mark Denby at News Books for putting up with my endless questions, enthusiasm, and presence over the past three months. I must record my appreciation to The Sunday Times, especially to John Jay for his help and advice, and to John Witherow for giving the go-ahead to this project. Finally thanks to all my friends and family for their support and understanding since the summer, when I disappeared to get this written. **RS**

Contents

Foreword

By John Jay
Business Editor

Tony Blair talks about trying to modernise Britain as a country that combines competitive enterprise with social justice. Without enterprise there can be no money for social justice and without entrepreneurs there can be no enterprise. Young and fast-growing companies are the source of much of the innovation and creativity in the modern British economy; the engines of both wealth and employment creation. A country that ignores its entrepreneurs quickly runs into trouble.

That is why when John Witherow, the editor of The Sunday Times, asked me to expand the small business section two years ago I developed a column called "My First Break" and asked Rupert Steiner, one of the newspaper's most enthusiastic young reporters, to become its author. My office bookshelves are full of dry management textbooks claiming to tell would-be entrepreneurs "how to" build a business. We instead set out through case studies to identify the well-springs of entrepreneurial activity.

The fact is that all aspiring business people need their breaks — the chance meeting, the breakthrough contract, the accidental stumbling on an original idea — and Rupert set out to capture these within a series of profile articles. Sometimes ambition drives entrepreneurs forward, sometimes intellectual arrogance — the "I can do it better" motive — but often adversity provides the vital spur and sometimes just plain boredom. Many people simply are uncomfortable working within big hierarchical organisations dominated by corporate politics and turf battles and want to get out on their own and prove that they "can do it".

In the post-war era corporatist governments from both left and right ignored the importance of entrepreneurship within society. Big was beautiful. Harold Wilson's white hot technological revolution was focussed on rationalising and reorganising industrial leviathans and the governments of Edward Heath and James Callaghan spent their time propping up lame ducks from a previous industrial era. But the recent history of America shows us how a combination of innovation, flexible labour markets and flexible capital markets can promote far more growth than any industrial strategy created by politicians or civil servants without any feel for markets and consumers.

When the men from Whitehall try to pick winners they almost always fail. That lesson is at best only partially understood in Britain. But the stories of the business people who feature in this book point the way forward — and may provide inspiration for a future generation of entrepreneurs, who driven by a will to win or some inner demon of insecurity, are willing to take risks and have a go at building their own enterprises.

Introduction

**By
Rupert Steiner**

As author of The Sunday Times My First Break column I am often asked "What's the secret to becoming an entrepreneur?" It is a virtually impossible question to answer. It is not like asking what makes a good accountant or lawyer where there is a set course and a structure, and where those who excel follow the procedures, sharpen their skills and play the game as part of a team. In the past two years I have interviewed more than 100 entrepreneurs and can only conclude that the most truthful answer is that there is no secret because there is no one path for entrepreneurs.

Entrepreneurs follow a different drum beat. They tend to be rebels, outsiders, and original thinkers who take risks and break new ground, constantly on the look-out for new opportunities. For them there is no right way and no wrong way to start a business. All that is needed is the guts to go out and do it. All entrepreneurs must take their first steps. They have to come up with good ideas they can execute better than anyone else, find a niche they can fill, secure the finance to build the infrastructure to make it happen and then keep it afloat until it starts to make a profit. Total commitment, even obsession, is required for success. Hard work, initiative, perseverance, determination and confidence are just the starting characteristics.

From where does the spark come? Sue Birley, Imperial College Management School Professor of entrepreneurship, thinks most people have the skills required even though only a few become business self-starters. "We all have it but some people just need to have it activated within them," says Birley. "Everyone sees an opportunity but the skill is turning that idea into a business and that requires persuasion, persistence and no inhibition about begging, borrowing and stealing resources to transform the vision into reality."

Others believe entrepreneurs are driven by specific psychological attributes and even flaws. Many have an all-consuming need to prove something to themselves and others, suffering deep-down from low self-esteem. Some are profoundly insecure, always trying to prove they are better than the opinion they hold of themselves. But they also tend to be insightful about others' strengths and weaknesses, with a gut feel for what their customers want, or think they want, and a talent for leading and motivating their staff.

Cary Cooper, Bupa Professor of organisational psychology at Manchester University's Institute of Science and Technology, has carried out extensive research into the subject. He says many are 'bounce-back people' with a powerful desire to achieve. They do not get distracted by either success or failure; they just plough on, never satisfied and constantly in fear of 'being found out'. Often after one success they think, 'I fooled them' and need to do it again to prove it was not just a freak event.

Failure is the same, according to Cooper. They see it as confirming inner fears but they do not give up: instead they pick themselves up and attempt to show they can get it right the second time around. Cooper says being an entrepreneur, even a successful one, has negative sides. Entrepreneurs often miss out on close relationships and the family life that middle managers can usually accommodate. Many reflect on this later in life but find themselves dazzled by business success like deer frozen in headlights. Many do not care about anything other than the business — it can be like a drug.

Beyond that it is difficult to typecast entrepreneurs. They walk along untrodden paths. Some stride forward with steely, unwavering determination that oozes from every pore. Others appear to blunder along, progressing almost by accident, driven by events rather than shaping them. Sometimes, it seems, a multi-million pound business has arrived out of nowhere.

Few appear like tycoons from central casting. Although some are flashy in the extreme and revel in the accumulation of 'boys' toys', many of the most successful avoid all conspicuous displays of wealth and cultivate an understated aura. Only a tiny few claim to have set out specifically to build big businesses and attain wealth. Cooper says the reason is that money is often not the prime driver. It becomes important but is often simply a way of keeping score, a means of beating off the inner demons: "We need to draw a distinction between 'real' entrepreneurs and the 'functional' variety.

"Functional entrepreneurs are ones who I do not class as genuine entrepreneurs. They have one good idea and live off that success. They like to be seen with their money because they have little drive to do it again, and need to show they have been successful."

'Real' entrepreneurs are motivated differently. They have to keep on coming up with new ideas to prove to themselves and their peers they can keep on doing it. They do not need Armani suits and Rolls Royces for enjoyment; they are driven more by fear of failure than lust for money. Functional entrepreneurs just do it for the money and then get out, often trading their businesses for country estates and the odd quango chairmanship. Real entrepreneurs can never stop.

The skills required to manage an existing business are quite different to those involved when someone plucks up the nerve to leave behind the comfort of a salary and start something from scratch with no guarantees. This is why so many entrepreneurs grow tired of their businesses after a while and sell them or recruit sufficient fresh managers to free them up from day-to-day involvement. Once the buzz from the original risk has faded, many are on the look out for their next entrepreneurial fix. They are by definition risk takers, modern merchant adventurers avoiding the stifling bureaucracy and politics of big companies. The dotting of every 'i' and crossing of every 't' they tend to leave to middle managers working to a structured game plan. Such people like to chart the life-cycles of their businesses because they fear the unknown. Unlike the entrepreneur, they find virgin territory unimaginable. They crave the security of operating within the rules.

Professor Birley says there are different types of entrepreneur and it is wrong to limit the term to those who come up with ideas: "Ideas are two a penny. It is how you make them work and translate them into viable businesses that counts. This involves constantly talking to people and listening to the market. Flexibility and making it up as you go along is the point."

Cooper says many entrepreneurs are incapable of actually running a business and often those who appear to be doing so have in fact delegated responsibility to a strong team of managers whose strengths and weaknesses they know: "They get a buzz from risk taking and pitching their judgement against the odds. They don't like the tedium of building a company. The clever ones choose a partner with whom they are compatible and the two supplement each others' 'weaknesses.'

Hugh Corbett, who started the Slug and Lettuce pub chain is a good example of a serial entrepreneur who is not solely interested in building a big business. He sold Slug and Lettuce to Grosvenor Inns for £2.5m and then built the Tup pub chain, which, no doubt, he will also try to sell: "I get a kick out of coming up with ideas and making them work. I'm no more than just a landlord who enjoys running pubs. I have no interest in worrying about bank managers, venture capitalists and the state of the property market. I can't even run a bath. I just don't like the day in, day out, routine involved with big business but I realise routine forms the skeleton of a successful business. I just don't need it."

Self-starting often means starting out as a teenage tycoon and learning the laws of supply and demand by trading in the playground. Richard Branson, Britain's best-known businessman, had a number of early money making schemes. In all of them he faced adversity that could have stopped him in his tracks. But Branson did not give up.

What sparked Branson's entrepreneurial drive? The answer may lie in his childhood. When he was four his mother left him by the side of the road and said: "It's time you became a man." By nightfall, Branson still had not made it home and a rescue crew had to be sent out. His mother would boast that one day he would be prime minister and she nagged him to "do something useful". He now says the idea of usefulness is what fires him.

Cooper believes entrepreneurs are driven by a need to control a world they could not control in their childhoods. In a survey he discovered many were inspired by a caring parent or a mentor. "My work confirmed earlier evidence that particularly the mother plays a most powerful role in establishing entrepreneurial action in the male child," he says. "More than 70% of entrepreneurs could identify some significant shaping event in their childhood." A factor common to many of the entrepreneurs Cooper has researched, and to some of those featured in this book, is the number who suffered bereavement at an early age. Psion's David Potter, whose father died when Potter was just 14, is but one example. Cooper reckons such people see themselves as "marginalised" and are thus driven to achieve. One businesswoman I interviewed told me: "When the worse thing imaginable hits you at such an early age and you survive it, there is little else in life that can be seen as a hurdle."

Branson says he probably would not have been able to start Virgin if he had not done so while still a teenager. He says: "The advantage was I had nothing to lose — no mortgage, no dependents, no ties. I had not yet become conservative and just got out there into the real world to try something to survive." Branson stresses the power of effective communication with staff. "Half my success is due to getting the right people around me and encouraging them to be committed to what I am doing," he says.

The key is looking at sectors or activities and seeing how one can do things differently even if it means flaunting conventional wisdom, something he calls "thinking out of the box". But intense interest is also vital. "It helps to have an excellent idea connected with a hobby," he says. "You are spending so much time with a business it makes all the difference to have a passion and interest in what you are doing. You won't make money unless you have a passion for what you do."

Bernie Ecclestone turned Formula One into a billion-pound business, and became Britain's sixth richest person according to The Sunday Times Rich List. He too was a teenage entrepreneur who grew up in humble surroundings in Dartford, Kent during the war. Aged nine and still living off rations, he would get up at dawn, fill a suitcase full of Chelsea buns from local bakers and sell them during the lunchbreak. He graduated to trading in fountain pens at 14 but today he claims luck was important in him becoming an entrepreneur. "Millions of people that work as hard or even harder than me are not as lucky as I've been. Luck has played a big part," he says. "I don't think any entrepreneur plans to be an entrepreneur. People just arrive at situations where something that looks good floats by and they have the balls to seize it, harness it and give it a go. Out of 100 entrepreneurs, 80 you never hear about, 18 fail, and two are really lucky and successful."

Ecclestone is uncomfortable talking about the origins of what became Formula One Holdings. But he does say trust, honesty and reputation were important. "Entrepreneurs need to be flexible, able to change direction at a moment's notice rather than sitting down with a board and coming up with reasons not to go for something," he says. "They need to be arrogant enough not to listen why they shouldn't do something. There are always people who haven't done anything who spend their lives warning others not to do things. But they are the ones who have missed the boat. All the businesses I have started are entrepreneurial. Then you get past that stage and either the entrepreneur becomes a businessman or you find a way of it being run like a business."

Most of the people in the book showed business flair as children, doing things such as selling worms to fishermen or hawking old football programmes from a stall. People do not typically switch on being an entrepreneur. They do not just wake up as would-be tycoons at 30. Some comes from nature, some from nurture. It is hard for people to be taught to be entrepreneurs: they either have it in their genes or in their upbringing or not at all. The reason is people cannot be taught to relish risk taking either based on research or gut feel; imagination is not typically picked up in the classroom.

But academics believe that education can help to provide those with a spark with at least some of the skills they will need to turn that spark into something more substantive. Michael Hay is director for the Foundation for Entrepreneurial Management at the London Business School. He says it is possible to give aspiring entrepreneurs some insight and help to build their confidence: "You can't give them an entrepreneurial injection but can take people with an element of entrepreneurial orientation and teach them a lot about getting a business off the ground. You can't teach people to have a good idea but you can develop inter-personal skills, sales, marketing and general management skills. You can make them better prepared and increase the odds for success." He says it is crude to say people are born entrepreneurs but thinks they are shaped by early experiences and role models.

What is constant is getting 'a break' — the one key move that has enabled the people in this book to start off on the road to success. These breaks can be roughly categorised and I have organised the chapters around such categories.

First there are the **Young Guns**, the teenage tycoons like Roger Saul, David Sullivan and Kevin Threlfall, who all started out selling products on market stalls in Britain. On the other side of the world, Masaya Nakamura, head of Namco, the company responsible for Pac-man and other electronic games, also started in a market in Japan, selling rides on a single rocking horse at the top of a department store.

The second chapter, **Rebels With A Cause**, delves into motivation, revenge, belligerence and a refusal to take 'no' for an answer, qualities often as important as the desire to make money. Michael Bloomberg was ejected from Salomon Brothers after telling the investment bank he could do things better and out of revenge he did just that for Merrill Lynch, Salomon's great rival. Raymond Blanc had to do better than his father. As a trainee he was hit in the face by a chef when he professed to know more than him. He picked himself up and went out to prove this and is now one of Britain's leading restaurateurs.

Good Connections and **My Brilliant Idea** are the themes of chapters three and four. Both are often vital to an entrepreneur's success. Pat McGovern started out as a journalist and through the contacts he established realised there was a demand for technological information. He now has a billion dollar publishing company, which includes the *PC World* magazine. No one can doubt Mike Gooley, founder of Trailfinders, and April Ducksbury, co-founder of Models One, did not come up with cracking ideas.

Finding **A Gap In The Market** is the subject of the fifth chapter. Jonathan Elvidge's Gadget Shops were started when he could not find any unusual presents for his family one Christmas. David Potter of Psion and Vision Express's Dean Butler also fall into this category.

The last two chapters focus on the entrepreneur's **Power Of Persuasion** and ability in **Raising The Stakes** (show me the money). Often people find it hard to raise capital for a good idea. Many get around this by embarking on a subsidiary activity to raise the cash for what they really have in mind. Laura Tenison is one such example. She went into a specialist estate agency to raise the seedcorn capital for her clothing business. Peter Stringfellow, the nightclub owner, puts his success down to persuasion. He convinced the local vicar to let him run dances in his church hall and then became the impresario behind a cabaret of semi-naked women.

The book is not a "how to" guide. It is a collection of vignettes written to satisfy the inquisitive who walk past Paul Smith, eat Virginia Lopalco's pasta, or use David Potter's Psion and wonder how they started that? But it does, I hope, remove some of the mystique surrounding starting a business and may inspire others to have a go.

Rupert Steiner
December 1998

Note: In the process of compiling this book, all interviews were reviewed to include each subject's most recent business ventures. Interviewees were also asked to complete a curriculum vitae. Although some of the CVs have been edited to conform to available space, the responses are reproduced as written.

1

Young Guns

Bernie Ecclestone
formula one

Justin Etzin
corporate events

David Sullivan
publishing

Roger Saul
fashion accessories

Kevin Threlfall
retailing

Gil Shwed
computer software

Chris Swan
car-parts distribution

Richard Branson
travel/leisure/finance

Formula One is formula for success

Original interview
13 December 1998

Bernie Ecclestone of Formula One fame is one of the world's great negotiators, a skill he has parlayed into a billion pound fortune.

Ecclestone, the king of grand prix motor racing, is a serial entrepreneur and workaholic who claims never to take holidays. In the 1950s he raced motorbikes and formula three cars and involved himself in a series of companies, but he sold or wound down all of his businesses in 1973 in protest at the introduction of VAT.

Then came his big break. The story of what became the Formula One Constructors' Association (FOCA) and Formula One Holdings (FOH) begins when he bought the assets of the troubled Brabham racing team and invested in new cars and drivers, including Graham Hill. Initially he did not take it seriously. "Basically it was a hobby," he says. "Ron Taranac, Jack Brabham's old partner, asked me to go into partnership with him and although I did not do this, I bought the team. I used to enjoy myself running it."

But tinkering with a hobby was not enough. Ecclestone missed the thrill of deal-making and saw an opportunity to move from running Brabham to organising the entire races. Other teams had tried to tap his expertise, asking him to help get Formula One into shape.

"It just sort of grew," he says. "And I got more and more stuck into it. I enjoyed the wheeler dealing side of it, I have always been a hustler. I had no idea where Formula One would take me. I have been lucky. It needed looking after and it wasn't being dealt with at all. I was in the right place at the right time. In the end I could not spend as much time as I wanted to at Brabham as I concentrated on getting FOCA off the ground."

Today he heads FOCA, FOH and a web of sister companies from a base in London's Knightsbridge. The principal activity of FOH, which is owned by trusts for the benefit of his wife, Slavica, and his two children, is the exploitation of television rights. It also controls the size of the prize fund and its distribution. At the outset FOCA won the rights to run Formula One in exchange for a licence fee and Ecclestone's team began transporting 50 cars, 600 people and 250 tons of freight around the world in jets for the races.

Date of Birth
November 1930

Nationality
British

Present Company
**Formula One Holdings and other
F1 Companies**

Age when first in business
18

Education
**Dartford School, Kent; Woolwich
Polytechnic**

Early entrepreneurial ventures
**Sold Chelsea buns from a
suitcase to kids in the
playground, aged 9. Bought and
sold fountain pens, aged 14**

School holiday job
Worked in a motorcycle shop

Qualifications
Some sort of Physics degree

First job
Trainee chemist at gas works

Sales/Profit before tax 1997
**Formula One Holdings is
valued at around £1.4 billion**

Weeks holiday per year
**Rarely take holidays. Have
Christmas off**

Hobbies/Sports/Interests
Like relaxing with my family

Idiosyncrasies, eg, car owned
Mercedes, Audi A4 Estate

**'You have an instinct.
You can't learn
business. I'm as
good as my word —
reputation counts
for everything.'**

Having sold Brabham he concentrated on Formula One full time, sitting on the board of the sports' ruling body and negotiating television transmission around the world. It became a hugely profitable venture, not least because Ecclestone spotted the potential of digital television long before others, spending £60m on sophisticated systems. In doing so he has created a spectacle that attracts a world-wide audience and global companies with budgets for multi-million pound sponsorship deals. In 1993 he was able to pay himself £29m, the highest salary ever recorded in Britain.

He now plans to float FOH, but is waiting for a green light from Brussels where the European Commission is probing his control over the sport. He is also, as a prelude to the float, issuing $2 billion of bonds secured on his revenue stream.

Ecclestone was born in Suffolk in 1930, he grew up in Bexleyheath, Kent with his parents and sister. Of his childhood and his early business ventures he has been silent in the past. But now has agreed, for the first time, to speak with The Sunday Times. His father was a trawler captain but did not own his boat. He went to Dartford School and was moderately academic. His first entrepreneurial move came at nine when he began exploiting wartime food shortages.

"I would get up bright and early in the morning and got friendly with the local baker, who let me fill a suitcase full of Chelsea buns, which I sold during the lunch break at school." At 14 he was buying and selling fountain pens.

His father let him leave school at 16 on condition that he worked for a friend, the local gas works' chief chemist. "I'd have done anything to leave school. There were better things to do outside." In his lunch hour he started to buy and sell motorcycles, which he advertised in the local paper and soon went to work in a Bexleyheath motorcycle shop. He was so successful that the owner made him a partner at 18. "I was doing deals and made enough money to team up with Fred Compton and started Compton & Ecclestone, which grew to be one of the largest motorcycle dealerships in Britain. I bought out Fred and then my old employer." He then diversified into cars, hire purchase and car auctions.

> **'His first business move came at nine when he exploited wartime food shortages.'**

Of entrepreneurship he says: "You have an instinct. You can't learn business. I'm as good as my word — reputation counts for everything. I always like to think that whatever deal you do you need to leave something for someone else. I would never screw someone right to the floor or take advantage of anyone in trouble."

Of retirement he says: "I will continue until I feel I am no longer doing a good job and perhaps letting others down."

Car wash kid polishes his act

**Original interview
8 March 1998**

Justin Etzin grasped basic economics while cleaning cars. But his rise to riches began as a teenage ball organiser.

Some entrepreneurs find themselves starting money-making schemes before they even reach their teens, but few are able to use their experiences to build a business turning over more than £1m by the time they reach 22.

Justin Etzin is one such example. He started at the age of 12 making £130 a weekend cleaning neighbours' cars. He moved on to a series of similar schemes before organising parties from a mobile phone in his dormitory at boarding school.

He founded Capital VIP, a business organising events, in 1994, and it became fashionable after arranging the teenage balls frequented by Prince William, and the Conservative party election bash. Other clients include Gucci, BT, Harrods, and Louis Vuitton. But his drive to become a teenage tycoon came from his father, who was involved in setting up Brother, the Japanese computer giant.

Etzin's first break came when his father offered him £2 to wash the family car, which set him thinking. He had picked up some basic business skills from evenings at home listening to his father haggle over deals. Etzin refused to clean his father's car for what he felt was a derisory amount, and went to work on a neighbour's, charging the princely sum of £5. "I used to watch how my father schmoozed people and saw he drove a tough deal. I wouldn't have been a chip off the old block if I hadn't tried to maximise my revenue."

Etzin got bored of car washing and while walking down London's Oxford Street noticed the huge trade hawkers were doing in posters. He thought if he could buy them for the right price, he could make a decent return selling them on the King's Road in Chelsea. He says: "I used the money from car washing to buy 100 posters off the hawker at a discounted price of £1 each, and just stood in front of this empty shop with the posters stuck to the window behind me selling them at £5 a go. I sold out by the end of the first day."

He beat his hawker-supplier down to 60p per poster for his stock, but then spotted the wholesaler's address at the bottom of the bag and approached the firm directly, managing to get the posters at a bargain price of 12p each. But Etzin began to get into trouble with the police who were concerned about his age, and the fact he had no licence to trade outside the shop. He overcame this by contacting the estate agents who were seeking tenants for the shop, and managed to secure a note on letter-headed paper stating he had permission to use the shop front.

Etzin claims he made thousands of pounds at weekends and after school selling the posters. But his biggest enterprise came in 1989 when he was sent to Bedales, a public school in Hampshire. He had a turbulent time because he rarely followed the rules and did barely enough work to pass his exams. But by the age of 15 he became restless. He says: "I was listening to the radio when they were auctioning a night in a wine bar for charity — it had only raised £200. I thought, if I filled it with 200 schoolfriends, put in a bid for £500 and charged £10 a go, I would walk away with £1,500. So I put in a bid."

But the wine bar refused because he was a teenager. However, his appetite had been whetted, and he approached the Ministry of Sound nightclub to rent the venue. He says: "The owners did not take me seriously at first, but I was able to put down the 10% deposit from money saved from my poster business. I then spread the word around the public-school circuit, and prayed. I needed to pay in full a week before the bash, and had only sold a handful of tickets — I calculated I

needed to sell only 300 tickets to break even, and managed to muster it a day before my deadline."

But word soon spread. More than 2,000 teenage revellers turned up and Etzin made £10,000 profit. He organised a further four balls in his first year using his mobile telephone as a box-office number, and later employed a friend to take the calls.

Capital VIP was formed and he started a degree at Oxford Brookes University, but he became bored and left to run the company full-time. He opened an

> **'I used to watch how my father schmoozed people and saw he drove a tough deal.'**

office in Fulham, employed two staff and made £50,000 profit in the first year. Etzin has a web of companies, one of which he wound up last year as part of restructuring. Capital VIP now employs 10 staff and its core business has become managing corporate events, which made £230,000 profit on sales of £700,000 for 1997.

Etzin is looking to float part of the business at the end of 1999. He says success is down to determination and not taking no for an answer: "If you want something badly enough you will get it in the end. The business I am in revolves around young people, so I am at an advantage, even if I don't have decades of business experience. I have more experience than people think — I started young."

'... even if I don't have decades of business experience, I have more experience than people think.'

Name: **Justin Etzin**

Date of Birth
12 February 1976

Nationality
British

Present Company
Capital VIP

Age when first in business
15

Education
Sussex House Prep School; Bedales Boarding School; Oxford Brookes University — however, did not complete degree course in European Business Studies

Early entrepreneurial ventures
Car washing

School holiday job
Washing cars at 12 years old and selling black & white 'arty' posters on the King's Road, Chelsea

Qualifications
10 GCSEs, 1 'A' level

First job
See School holiday job above

Sales/Profit before tax 1997
Turnover: anticipated c£1.5m 1998

Weeks holiday per year
Many business trips abroad — pleasure thrown in wherever possible

Hobbies/Sports/Interests
Tennis, skiing, riding, and making money

Idiosyncrasies, eg, car owned
BMW 328i convertible; religiously buying The Sunday Times on my way home on a Saturday night/early Sunday morning after clubbing; a PR agent; vodka and cranberry juice; a Nokia mobile phone/fax/organiser; the size of the Rock of Gibralter; a 21-year-old teddy bear, stocks, shares & bonds

Programmed for the big time

Original interview
12 October 1997

At 12, David Sullivan learnt about marketing by selling old football fanzines. Now he owns Birmingham City and Sport Newspapers.

David Sullivan's lust for football, publishing and making money had become a part of his life before he had even reached his teens. He cut his entrepreneurial teeth at 12, selling football programmes to supplement his pocket money. He would persuade football clubs to let him have old programmes for free and then bundle them together and market them through soccer magazines. By the time he reached 18, he had made £3,000 — enough to buy a new Ford Capri and pay the deposit on a flat in east London.

He had also picked up the basics of marketing and whetted his appetite for starting his own business. The brazen cheek Sullivan showed with his first enterprise — selling something that had cost him nothing — has become synonymous with the way he does business.

Sullivan has built an empire around spotting an opportunity. He made a fortune from soft pornography, owning men's magazines and sex shops. Then he founded the Sunday Sport newspaper. He is also chairman of Birmingham City, the AIM company that owns the football club in which he invested £9m in 1993. In 1997, Sullivan made £20m from his group of companies — Sport Newspapers made a profit of £9.3m on sales of £25m and he is looking to diversify into mainstream film production.

He is the 93rd richest man in Britain, according to The Sunday Times Rich List, with a fortune of £200m. His Essex mansion and stud are thought to be worth £10m. But this sprawling empire is a far cry from his boyhood trading in football programmes, which Sullivan says sparked his interest in publishing. "It was a hobby I turned into a business," he says. "I collected programmes and so did my friends. I would go along to football clubs and ask for any old remainders and fill up my dad's van.

"I would bundle up 50 different programmes and sell them as starter packs. People would get one or two from each season and want to buy the rest from me to complete the series. Basic marketing — it was very good grounding." He adds: "My dad was an officer

'It is a British disease
to accept failure too
readily and give up.
In life, if you fail,
walk away and find a
new opportunity.'

Date of Birth
5 February 1949

Nationality
British

Present Company
**Roldvale Ltd, Sport Newspapers,
Birmingham City**

Age when first in business
11

Education
**Abbs Cross Technical School,
Hornchurch (11-16); Watford
Grammar School (16-18); Queen
Mary College, London University
(19-21)**

Early entrepreneurial ventures
**Selling football programmes
by mail order and from stalls
outside soccer grounds**

School holiday job
**Worked for two years (16-17) at
Bartons Bakery, Chadwell Heath**

Qualifications
**Grad 1 'A' levels (plus 2 'S' levels)
in Politics & Economics, Maths &
Statistics, History; Honours
Graduate & Economics Scholar,
London University**

First job
**Assistant account executive in
advertising**

Sales/Profit before tax 1997
Approximately £20m profits

Weeks holiday per year
Two to three weeks

Hobbies/Sports/Interests
**Football, boxing, racing, films,
politics, current affairs**

Idiosyncrasies, eg, car owned
**Always buy British, hence a
Bentley**

in the RAF and we lived on bases. He was terrified he'd be thrown out of the services for running a business, which was not allowed.

"I've always had a total belief I'd make money in whatever I did. I guess this early start reinforced my confidence and it set me thinking about building my own business. People are born with skills; mine is making money."

Sullivan studied economics at London University. After graduating he joined an advertising agency, where he worked on pet-food accounts. But he was not happy, and after six months he joined another agency where he worked for Gerald Ronson's Heron group.

"I spent every Monday afternoon touring petrol stations with Gerald," says Sullivan. "He was ferocious to work for, but really quite brilliant and knew how to drive people. He was the ultimate promoter, a brilliant test marketer who would make plenty of mistakes, but enough right decisions for it not to matter."

Sullivan was on a salary of £1,750 and started to look for ways of supplementing his income. He had read an article about how Bob Guccione had started Penthouse after selling pictures of topless girls through Exchange & Mart. He decided to give it a go himself and teamed up with Bernard Hardingham, a university friend. They put up £100 each and hired a photographic studio where they took photos of women friends. Through mail order, they sold packs of 20 pictures for £1 and also produced one of the first sex-educa-

tion manuals, which was advertised in the Observer and The Sunday Times.

Sullivan claims this was not a line of business he was familiar with. "I was very naive, I had hardly ever seen a girlie book," he says. "But it was basic marketing. I tapped a combination of what I had learnt selling football programmes and test-marketing advertisements for Ronson.

"The advantage of mail order is that you instantly see which advertisements work. I left my job after we started making £2,000 a week on the back of marketing the products by classified advertising, but Bernard sold his stake

> **'It was a hobby I turned into a business. I collected programmes and so did my friends.'**

in the business because of objections from his wife. In 18 months I made £300,000 and Bernard left his wife."

Sullivan expanded into sex shops, opening 139 in two years. He also invested in property and made some feature films. By the time he was 30, he was making £1m a year, and in 1986 he realised his ambition to start a newspaper — the Sunday Sport.

He says his success is down to taking knocks in his stride. "It is a British disease to accept failure too readily and give up. In life, if you fail, walk away and find a new opportunity. There is nothing to lose."

Street trading bears fruit for Mulberry's Saul

**Original interview
24 August 1997**

Roger Saul, founder of Mulberry, the luxury leather accessories company, got his grounding from a tough old trader in a London street market.

Roger Saul started his business career as a schoolboy entrepreneur caught up in the buzz of 1960s. As a 16-year-old boarder at school in Bath, he travelled to London's Portobello Road at weekends to trade old military uniforms from a market stall.

The uniforms were the height of fashion and Saul wanted to make enough money to kit himself out in the latest gear. But his ambition grew and soon he was designing and making belts in a garden shed.

Three years after starting a small business making leather accessories, Saul formed Mulberry with £500 given to him by his parents. Since then it has become Britain's top maker of leather accessories and an international brand. Mulberry was floated on the Alternative Investment Market in May 1996 and the following year was valued at £29m, with profits of £1.7m on a turnover of £31.6m.

It has 52 outlets from Tokyo to Helsinki and employs 550 people selling accessories, clothing and home furnishings. Saul has diversified and opened a country hotel but plans for a similar venture in London and a restaurant chain have been put on ice.

His passion for fashion dates back to his school days. A boarder at Kingswood, Bath, he would change from his school uniform to second-hand clothes for Saturday night dances in London.

Saul's first break came when a Welsh market trader called Bob Pandy took him under his wing. "I bought a uniform from him at Portobello market and we got talking," he says. "I came back a week later and asked him to let me have a corner of his stall to buy and sell uniforms. He was a real tough old trader and I think he was amused by this enthusiastic public-school boy trying to make a go of what he did. I guess he was flattered by my interest and persistence."

Pandy was selling second-hand wolf coats and silver fox furs to stars like The Beatles and The Rolling Stones. Saul was thrilled. Soon he was picking up selling and negotiating skills. He says: "It was awe-inspiring to learn from Pandy after leading a pretty sheltered life. There was a buzz to going out trading, learning how to survive, and putting yourself at risk. This was what it was all about."

When Saul left school he worked with Pandy and took a business studies course at Westminster College, London, with sponsorship from a solid-fuel distributor. He realised that his future did not lie there and convinced John Michael, the Carnaby Street trader, to sponsor him instead.

Saul expanded into designing belts and chokers from snake skin. He bought a knife and sewing machine and cut out designs that his girlfriend stitched together.

He soon developed a cult reputation, getting Biba and other boutiques to sell his goods. "It was the 1960s; anything was possible," says Saul. "But whether you succeeded was another matter."

Succeeding meant choosing between work and study, and he pulled out of his course in the last term to concentrate on design. His sister thought up the Mulberry emblem. "I needed something to capture what we were about, to compete with the likes of Pierre Cardin," he says. "A Mulberry is a tree of life; it bears fruit and is a great wood."

Business started slowly, with Saul selling belts to department stores from a suitcase and taking the orders back to Somerset, where they were made up by local craftsmen in a converted blacksmith's shed. In the first year,

sales were just £15,000 but after two years the business took off. By 1979 the company had expanded into America and Japan and was making £225,000 on sales of £1.4m, although it suffered badly in the recession of the early 1980s.

In 1992 Saul sold a quarter of the equity to Kleinwort Benson, Charterhouse and Phoenix for £4m and built a £2m factory.

He says the key to success is to approach everything from the customer's perspective. "Appreciating the different cultures is important," he

> **'I think he was amused by this enthusiastic public school boy trying to make a go of what he did. I guess he was flattered by my interest and persistence.'**

says. "Otherwise, grit, determination, and a belief in yourself and the product count for a lot. I like the team to enjoy their successes, and I make them think we are on a mission that is almost impossible. It makes for a more exciting ride where people can become more involved."

Date of birth
25 July 1950

Nationality
British

Present Company
Mulberry

Age when first in business
20

Education
Kingswood School, Bath; City of Westminster College, London

Early entrepreneurial ventures
Buying and selling Victorian military uniforms whilst at school

School holiday job
Clearing forests for The Forestry Commission; working in a London fashion boutique

Qualifications
'O' and 'A' levels at school. Then a Business Studies sandwich course with John Michael, fashion guru

First job
Mulberry

Sales/Profit before tax 1997
Sales: £31,673,000 Profit: £1.7m

Weeks holiday per year
Six weeks

Hobbies/Sports/Interests
Garden and interior design; skiing; racing historic cars; tennis. We have sponsored Mulberry Historic Car Grand Prixs and the Mulberry Classic at Hurlingham, a major tennis tournament

Idiosyncrasies, eg, car owned
I drive a 1956 Mercedes Gull-Wing, but more usually a Range Rover.

'Otherwise, grit, determination, and a belief in yourself and the product count for a lot. I like the team to enjoy their successes.'

Success in store for barrow boy

Original interview
4 January 1998

Kevin Threlfall inherited his passion for retailing from his parents and went on to build a market stall into a £140m empire.

Kevin Threlfall learnt about entrepreneurship at his mother's knee. She used to sell hot dogs round the pubs in Wolverhampton. "For every five she sold, she made an extra one by chopping off their ends and putting them together," says Threlfall. "So profits increased by 20%."

Threlfall digested this well — and learnt other lessons from his equally enterprising father. Today, he runs one of the larger retail businesses in the UK. The company he founded, T&S Stores, comprises 500 Dillons convenience stores, 320 newsagents and 180 branches of Supercigs. The group is valued at £140m and in 1997 made profits of £18m on sales of £500m.

Threlfall picked up his passion for retailing from his father, who started a business discounting tea and sugar when retail-price maintenance was abolished in the 1960s. "As a 10-year-old, I would go out with him whenever I could and I learnt his sales techniques. He wasn't good at maths so I loved to add up the bills quicker than he could."

But Threlfall junior soon developed his own entrepreneurial streak and teamed up with David Lockett-Smith, a friend with a vehicle-body repair business. They would spend the evenings refurbishing old caravans that they bought for £100. Threlfall's mother was roped in to sell the vehicles at £250 each by pretending each was a much-loved family holiday home — something she carried off more than 100 times.

Threlfall moved further into business after a set of disappointing exam results at Denstone College, Staffordshire. "I didn't get enough 'A' levels to go to university but found a course in Canada where my grades were good enough. I decided to wait a year for a friend who wanted to study with me."

Threlfall set about finding a job to fill the gap year. He rented a stall at Cannock market, selling groceries and household goods, and made £100 a week. But the one year turned into four when his friend failed his 'A' levels and Threlfall stayed in England. "The stall was just a temporary thing to earn some money but I ended up stuck with it as a career." He was concerned it had no future. So he started looking for a way to expand out of the market. The

Date of Birth
29 September 1948

Nationality
British

Present Company
T&S Stores Plc

Age when first in business
10

Education
Denstone College, Uttoxeter, Staffordshire

Early entrepreneurial ventures
Selling pet food door-to-door, working markets, selling caravans

School holiday job
Working markets

Qualifications
—

First job
Working markets

Sales/Profit before tax 1997
Sales: £500m Profit: £18m

Weeks holiday per year
Six weeks

Hobbies/Sports/Interests
Golf, flying, tennis and watching Wolverhampton Wanderers football team

Idiosyncrasies, eg, car owned
Aston Martin DBT

'Being a successful entrepreneur is down to a genetic cocktail and it helps to have commitment, hard work and common sense.'

stall served as an excellent training ground for future forays.

In the early 1970s, Threlfall heard that Kwik Save had set up in Wales and was making large profits from selling products at a 20% discount by buying in bulk from wholesalers. He wanted to do something similar. He looked around for a warehouse, and after two years found an old factory close to Wolverhampton market with a big car park. He had built up a relationship with Ralph Feeney, the owner of a local cash-and-carry and his main supplier. Threlfall approached Feeney for help to fund his idea.

"I was only 23 and already one of his biggest customers," he says. "Feeney knew I had entrepreneurial sparkle and decided to back me. The venture was going to cost £50,000 and Feeney was prepared to put up half. I had little means, and not sufficient to raise my half. He ended up lending me £5,000 and I borrowed another £5,000 from Barclays to buy a 20% stake."

In March 1972 his first shop, called simply Lo-Cost discount store, opened its doors. It was a larger version of Threlfall's market stall. He stuck prices on boxes, piled them high and sold them cheap. The staff soon grew from an initial 10 to 20. In its first year the store made a £10,000 profit. The most popular part of the shop was a kiosk selling discount cigarettes that worked on margins of just 1p. It brought in customers who then had to walk round the whole store to get to the exit. This yielded further sales of items that caught their eye. The concept was a success, and Threlfall began to roll out more stores, eventually building up a chain of 18. He started a separate business, called Supercigs, selling discount cigarettes in small kiosks, and had eight by 1977. Oriel Foods then offered to buy Lo-Cost for £1.6m, which Threlfall — whose share amounted to £280,000 — found too good to turn down.

Lo-Cost was making £300,000 on sales of £18m when he sold it. Threlfall now concentrated on building Supercigs, and decided to expand into discount sweets and cards, creating a branch of newsagents under an umbrella company called T&S Stores.

> **'As a 10-year-old, I would go out with my father whenever I could and I learnt his sales techniques.'**

This floated on the Unlisted Securities Market in 1984 with 56 stores. He followed the float with a series of acquisitions — in 1987 he bought 87 Buy-Wise stores, and in 1989 he bought 395 Preedy/Dillons stores from Next for £54m.

T&S moved to the main market in 1987. He says that success is in the blood: "You can't make yourself ambitious, it's either there or it's not. Being a successful entrepreneur is down to a genetic cocktail and it helps to have commitment, hard work and common sense."

Army fuelled fire to wage war on hackers

Original interview
13 July 1997

Overseeing sensitive files during national service inspired computer whiz kid Gil Shwed to devise a way of keeping systems data secure.

Gil Shwed became obsessed with computers before he reached his teens. He began computer classes at 10 and started writing programs a year later. By the time he was 13 he was earning $500 as a consultant to an Israeli software company. Sixteen years on, he is chief executive of his own software company, Check Point Software Technologies, which is valued at almost $1 billion (£625m) on Nasdaq. Shwed founded it in 1993 and floated it in June 1996 in a deal that made him worth $130m on paper. In 1997 he became Israel's young entrepreneur of the year.

Check Point Software Technologies is the market leader in 'firewall security software' products that are designed to protect computer systems against hackers. It has sold 60,000 programs worldwide so far, shipping them out through a sophisticated distribution system. With its products selling at between $10,000 and $20,000 each, Check Point has grown fast. It made profits of $30,000 in the first six months of 1994 on sales of $1m.

A year later the profits had risen to $5m. In 1997, the company's profits hit $40m on sales of $83m. Shwed spent most of his childhood stuck in front of a computer screen, but it was a stint in the Israeli army that set him thinking about starting his own business. "I spent four years doing national service and managed to spend it in the army computing department," he says. "I was exposed to a lot of security issues where there was sensitive information, which was classified and only accessible by certain ranks. I got to understand the different issues where everyone had to work on the same network but with different rights.

"Since the early days in the army I had an idea to create something. It was never very exciting working for someone else, which is how I spent most of my teenage years. I had this idea to create a product based around providing security for computer networks but I evaluated it with my friends and decided there was no market for it."

Shwed left the army to become a consultant, designing software for Orbotech, a computer company. He learnt how to create, package and market new products, and after a year noticed the Internet was taking off and companies were looking at how to connect securely. He approached two army friends, Shlomo Kramer, and Marius Nacht, who helped form the idea.

"It was a growth market and looked exciting," he says. "We understood two things: timing was important, we needed to be quick to be successful; and apart from mastering the technology it was essential to identify the sort of firms that needed our product."

Shwed drew up a business plan and approached some of the firms with which he had worked. They were interested and put up $300,000. It took the three of them four months to design a solution, using computers lent by Sun Microsystems. Shwed started to test the system at night on computer networks and had instant success. "Within one hour someone tried to break into the system, even though it was the first time these companies had ever been externally linked. The alarm sounded and we thought it can't be possible but two weeks later the police were able to make an arrest. It was a good confirmation for us."

In June 1993 Shwed formed the company around the product and agreed distribution and installation rights. It proved itself in a high-profile television test when two hackers were given 12 hours to break the system. Shwed had not bargained on the international hacking community joining in — the product survived 60,000 attempts to rubbish his technology.

Shwed grew up in Jerusalem, the son of a computer systems analyst, and went to the Betha Hayled school from where he regularly escaped to attend computer classes at a nearby university.

"I didn't like school and was already going to proper university classes at the age of 14," he says. "They let me work in my holidays designing computer systems for the chemistry department. I already had a job designing software for Scientific Translation International in the evenings."

> **'We understood timing was important, we needed to be quick to be successful.'**

He claims he is not motivated purely by money. "I was always curious about how things worked and wanted to understand the full picture," he says. "We spent a lot of time thinking and looked at our strengths and weaknesses. We realised our strength was not in selling but in designing and developing. Personal skills are critical, as is a drive to work hard. It is all very well having an idea, but making it happen and keeping it going is what counts. My childhood was rather ordinary although I never got a degree — I had attended all the courses I was interested in before I left school."

Date of Birth
—

Nationality
Israeli

Present Company
Check Point Software Technologies

Age when first in business
13

Education
Some University classes

Early entrepreneurial ventures
—

School holiday job
System Manager and computer programmer

Qualifications
None

First job
Computer programmer

Sales/Profit before tax 1997
Sales: $83m Profit: $40,208,000

Weeks holiday per year
One week

Hobbies/Sports/Interests
Rest and travel

Idiosyncrasies, eg, car owned
VW Beetle; Renault Clio

'It is all very well having an idea, but making it happen and keeping it going is what counts.'

Boyhood efforts put Swan in the saddle

**Original interview
16 February 1997**

The head of a £500m car-parts giant started as a 12-year-old bicycle restorer.

Chris Swan began his business career as a schoolboy, buying run-down bicycles, renovating them, and selling them on. "I was 12 years old and out of pocket," says Swan, chairman of Finelist, Britain's largest car-parts distributor.

"I would advertise to buy bikes in the local free paper and respray them, take the brakes out, clean them and do the same for the gears and chain. I would then sell the bike in a quality paid-for paper where I could command a premium. I loved the mechanics of replacing the parts and making money through giving customers what they wanted. I was buying, selling, marketing, and trading — not very different from what I do now. I would tend to buy bikes at £7, turn them round in six weeks, and sell them for £42 — tops. This led me to my first opportunity when I was 16 years old."

Swan was buying paint in Halfords one afternoon when he saw an advertisement for a Saturday job in the store where he could use what he had learnt in his bicycle business.

"I had an interview and my enthusiasm won me the job," he says. "I worked my summers there and spent my £3 daily wage on doing up my bikes. I really enjoyed meeting people and giving advice on radios and car parts, also helping to fit them. This gave me a focus, something to work towards."

Years later, Swan remains a believer in service and customer relations. He tells of how he once celebrated closing a business deal by visiting a Ferrari showroom. He asked a sneering salesman how the seat adjusted on one model and was marched round to the rear of the car and shown the badge. "Look sir," said the salesman. "You only buy this car if you want to say you've arrived."

He walked out of that Ferrari garage faster than the salesman could accelerate its 470bhp engine. "This shows just how important people are in business," says Swan, who says Finelist succeeds by motivating its 8,000 staff. "The trick is never to make an assumption about your customer. Understanding them is the key," he says.

Two weeks after his run-in with the Ferrari salesman, Swan spent £200,000 on a Jaguar XJ220 — one of just 68 on

Date of Birth
2 May 1958

Nationality
British

Present Company
Finelist Group Plc

Age when first in business
12 and out of pocket

Education
12 'O' levels, Coventry School

Early entrepreneurial ventures
Buying run-down bicycles, renovating them and selling them on

School holiday job
£3 per day at Halfords

Qualifications
Turned down place at Bath University to read Maths

First job
Management trainee at Halfords

Sales/Profit before tax 1997
Sales: £228.9m 1997, £388.1m 1998

Weeks holiday per year
Not many

Hobbies/Sports/Interests
All sports and keep-fit. Playing cricket and watching Derby County football team

Idiosyncrasies, eg, car owned
Jaguar XJ220

'Running a business is like owning an expensive car. It won't perform unless you know how to control and fuel it.'

the road and more than double the price of a Ferrari. He now takes pleasure in driving it past the Ferrari garage.

Swan grew up in Kenilworth, Warwickshire, one of three boys. His father was a polytechnic lecturer, his mother a tax officer. After getting 12 'O'-levels he joined the Halfords management-training scheme, turning down the chance to read maths at Bath University, and he was made a branch manager at 19.

He left soon after to join Brown Brothers, a car-parts distributor, as a salesman, and worked his way up to district manager. In 1983, aged 26, he joined Partco, a competitor, as south-east regional manager. It was sold to management in 1986 but Swan was too junior to take part, and realised he would never have a stake in the firm. After three years he left. "I've always been motivated by knowing what I want to achieve and not letting anyone stand in my way," says Swan. "I've never dodged a decision or looked back and thought 'What if'."

He combines determination with a love of the car industry, having worked his way up from Halfords to Brown Brothers and Partco.

His biggest break came when he joined Autela as operations manager and took part in the company's first management buyout (MBO) in 1989 from BBA, the conglomerate. Later he led a second MBO with venture-capital backing, with most of the equity coming from 3i and NatWest. "I had to do

it to see if I could," he says.

This unassuming man with a neat moustache and an enthusiastic handshake has arrived. Finelist Group gained a full listing in 1994, when it was valued at £28m, and in the same year it bought its closest rival, Edmunds Walker, for £19m. It is now worth £500m, was a finalist in the 1997 PLC Awards and Swan won the 1997 Entrepreneur of the Year award.

"In our sector it helps to have worked up from the bottom. I never get my staff to do anything I haven't done

> **'The trick is never to make an assumption about your customer. Understanding them is the key.'**

myself. I succeed through developing a team, looking after them financially, and encouraging them. I have always been determined to succeed and find setting unrealistic goals a great way of achieving the unachievable.

"Money is not my driver. I get a buzz out of building the company and looking into the future as much as possible to give customers what they need. Running a business is like owning an expensive car. It won't perform unless you know how to control and fuel it."

Late delivery causes Virgin birth

**Original interview
29 November 1998**

Selling a product more cheaply than the established provider is a classic way to enter a business and Richard Branson is one of the most successful exponents of the art.

First he did it with music, then airline travel and now he is involved in a big push into financial services while at the same time diversifying into rail transport, cinemas, cola, vodka, jeans and cosmetics. The story of how Branson became a billionaire begins as a tale of teenage entrepreneurship. It starts with *Student*, a magazine that Branson started as a 15-year-old pupil at Stowe. He left to run it from a friend's basement in Connaught Square, London. "I originally wanted to edit the mag but I found I was sinking more into being a businessman, organising advertising, distribution and marketing, which all took up more of my time than editing.

"I had always wanted to work for myself. It's a great luxury. But my only ambition was to be a journalist. I had no aspiration to be an entrepreneur. I just wanted to make enough to pay the bills and keep *Student* going."

That all changed when the young Branson spotted the growth in pop music sales in the mid-1960s and the opportunity created for price cutting when established stores failed to react to the ending of retail price maintenance by being more competitive.

Initially Branson sold cut-price records by mail order through *Student*. "There was a tremendous excitement about music. We had a flood of inquiries and more cash than we had ever seen before. We came up with the Virgin name because we knew we were Virgins at business."

But a postal strike threatened the embryonic Virgin and Branson set about finding a shop. "There was a strike, which lasted for two months, and I was forced to find an alternative means to sell records," he says. "I moved away from publishing and expanded into retailing." An instinctive retailer, Branson realised location was everything and set about doing his research, spending a morning comparing the number of shoppers in Oxford Street with those in Kensington High Street. Oxford Street won and he began hunting for a site near Tottenham Court Road tube station.

He saw a shoe shop with a stairway leading up to what looked like an empty first floor and used his legendary

39

marketing skills to persuade the owner to let him occupy it rent free until a paying tenant came along. His line was that the shoe shop would sell shoes to Virgin customers. He then put piles of cushions on the floor, carried a couple of old sofas up the stairs, set up a till and handed out fliers. He had a queue stretching 100 yards when it opened and never looked back.

A year on Branson opened a recording studio in an Oxfordshire country house, where musicians could make music in a relaxed informal atmosphere. His seed capital came from his parents, his Auntie Joyce and Coutts Bank.

In 1972 Virgin released its first record, Tubular Bells, by Mike Oldfield, and he then steadily expanded, making his biggest diversification move, the Virgin Atlantic airline in 1984.

For 1997, Branson claims that Virgin and all its associate companies collectively made profits of £150m on sales of £3 billion although a number of them are loss-making.

The son of a barrister, Branson grew up near Guildford, Surrey, and was sent to Scaitcliffe, a prep school. He had a number of playground money making schemes. At 14, he decided to plant Christmas trees to sell but rabbits ate into his profits when the trees were saplings and the crop failed. Pests again ruined his next venture, which was breeding budgerigars — they were all eaten by rats.

Branson was not academic and was more interested in journalism. "I wanted to set up an alternative magazine with a fresh attitude. I wanted to campaign against fagging, corporal punishment, games and Latin, and these ideas were far too revolutionary for the school magazine.

"I roped in some friends and linked up with other schools with similar rules, and created a list of advertisers from the telephone book and wrote to WH Smith asking whether they would be prepared to stock the magazine."

With advertisers, distributors and costs in place, Branson wrote his first business plan. His mother lent him £4 as a float against the cost of phone calls and letters and the father of a friend printed headed notepaper.

> **'We came up with the Virgin name because we knew we were Virgins at business.'**

Branson used the school pay phone to make calls and convinced the operator to give him free calls when he pretended he had lost his money in the machine. He would be connected and introduced as "Mr Branson," the operator sounded like a secretary. He reckons young entrepreneurs can take risks because they have no commitments. "There was nothing to lose and I had not started to be conservative," he says. "My principal skills are being good with people, finding a different way to do things and having a passion for what I do."

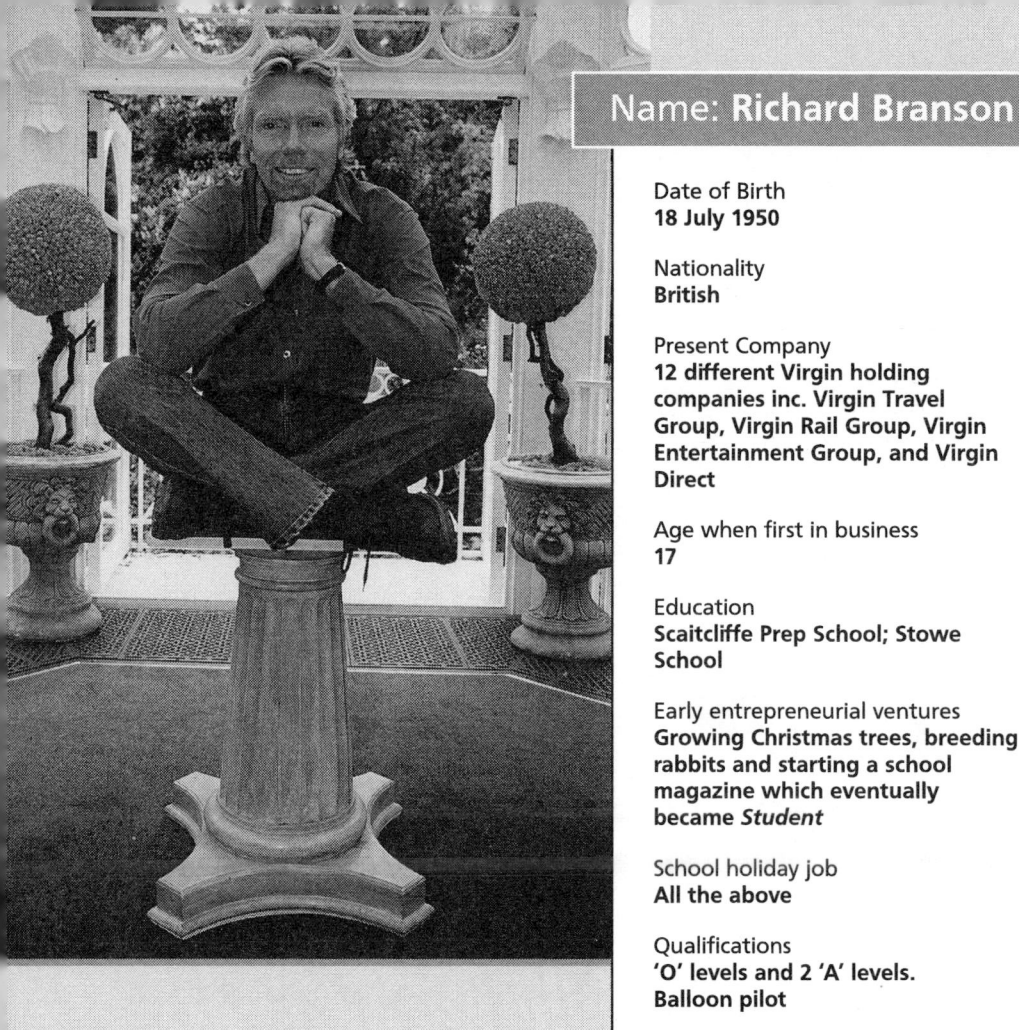

Date of Birth
18 July 1950

Nationality
British

Present Company
12 different Virgin holding companies inc. Virgin Travel Group, Virgin Rail Group, Virgin Entertainment Group, and Virgin Direct

Age when first in business
17

Education
Scaitcliffe Prep School; Stowe School

Early entrepreneurial ventures
Growing Christmas trees, breeding rabbits and starting a school magazine which eventually became *Student*

School holiday job
All the above

Qualifications
'O' levels and 2 'A' levels. Balloon pilot

First job
Publisher and Editor of *Student* magazine

Sales/Profit before tax 1997
All the Virgin companies in 1997 put together: Sales: £3 billion Profit: £150m

Weeks holiday per year
Six to seven, usually spent on Necker Island with the family

Hobbies/Sports/Interests
Ballooning, tennis, chess, scuba diving, perudo

Idiosyncrasies, eg, car owned
Not a car fanatic, own a 1976 Bristol. Monocyclist and occasional magician

'My principal skills are being good with people, finding a different way to do things and having a passion for what I do.'

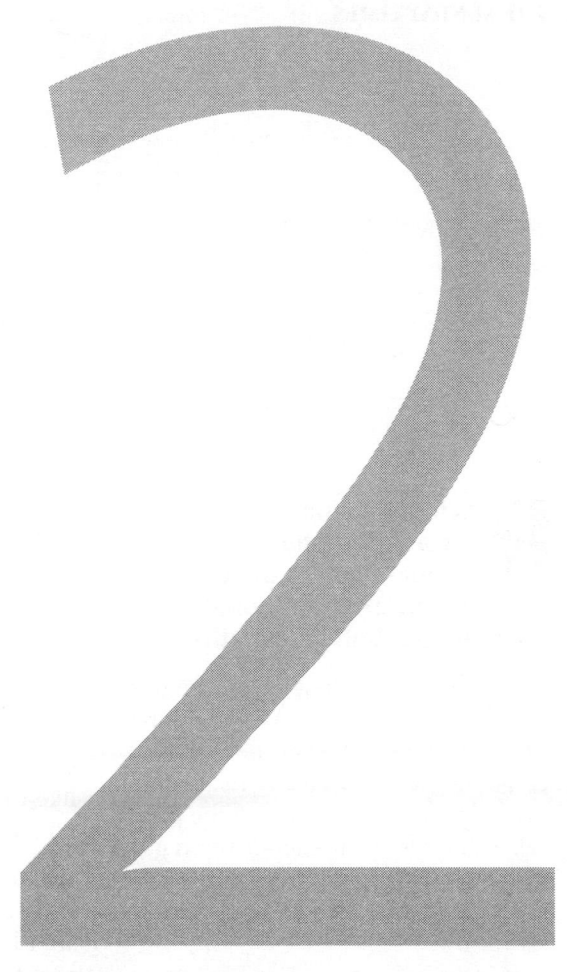

Rebels With A Cause

Raymond Blanc
restaurants

Michael Bloomberg
financial services

Andy Baker
recruitment

Cliff Hardcastle
electronic components

Hunt for perfection keeps Blanc hungry

**Original interview
8 June 1997**

Raymond Blanc, the restaurateur, hotelier and businessman, is driven by fear of the mediocrity that haunted his talented, but unfulfilled father.

Raymond Blanc's first adventure in the kitchen was a disaster. As a 17-year-old trying to impress his mother with crêpe Suzette he used a Pyrex dish instead of a metal pan to fry the pancakes. Shards of caramel-covered glass flew everywhere as it exploded with the heat. He decided cooking was not for him.

Thirty years on, Blanc has built a mini-industry around his kitchen, with cookery books, brasseries, and a country-house hotel. His businesses have sales of more than £10m a year and employ 250 staff. Still not satisfied, he retains ambitious expansion plans. His life is devoted to food. A diet of fear and determination made Blanc one of Britain's top chefs and a successful entrepreneur.

The son of a clockmaker, Blanc grew up in Besançon, near Dijon, with four brothers and sisters. "My father had a wonderful talent for working gold, and could have been the most brilliant jewellery designer," says Blanc.

"He was ambitious but could not bring himself to take a risk or dare, and has to live his life knowing he has never achieved his potential. Being unable to express the best from inside made him bitter. Because of his own failure my father wanted us to have a tremendous future. His failure was an important lesson for me. I never wanted to be like that and began to fear being mediocre."

Blanc felt under pressure to go into business and fell out with his father after he failed to complete his training as a draughtsman. "My father did not talk to me for two years and I wasn't allowed to come home because he thought I'd squandered my chances," he says.

Blanc tried various jobs, working in a factory and a garage and as a nurse. But at 21 he discovered a real interest in cooking after looking through a restaurant window and seeing a chef flambé sea bass. "I decided: 'That's it, I want to be a chef' and went to tell the restaurant owner the next day," he says.

"He did not warm to my confidence and offered me a job washing up. I eventually became a waiter. I began to educate myself and realised the chef

Date of Birth
19 November 1949

Nationality
French

Present Company
Le Manoir aux Quat'Saisons

Age when first in business
28 in 1977 with Les Quat'Saisons, Summertown, Oxford

Education
Statutory French education. No formal training for profession. Experience and expertise grew from intuition, enhanced by experimenting and accumulating technical experience.

Early entrepreneurial ventures
Les Quat'Saisons, Summertown, Oxford in 1977 and Maison Blanc (Patisserie/Boulangerie) in 1978

School holiday job
—

Qualifications
—

First job
—

Sales/Profit before tax 1997
**Turnover not discussed.
Profit before tax: £715,000**

Weeks holiday per year
—

Hobbies/Sports/Interests
Reading, music, tennis and swimming

Idiosyncrasies, eg, car owned
—

'Entrepreneurs should never feel there are limits. I have never formally trained as a chef or a businessman. The key is to go beyond the barriers and reinvent yourself.'

lacked creativity, and the meals were too salty. I told him this. But chef was God — even the owner was frightened of him. From one end of the kitchen he picked up a copper pan and threw it at me — breaking my nose and jaw."

The flying pot did not deter Blanc, but he decided he needed a change of scene before launching his own business. Thus when the owner visited him in hospital and told him of a job in England in the kitchens at the Rose Revived in Newbridge, near Oxford, he seized the opportunity. He soon realised Britain's food was poor.

"All the girls called me 'love,' and the food and wine were terrible," he says. "It was a country with no sensuality. These were dark times. The chef used to overcook the food with too many spices and often prepared the dishes a week in advance. But I learnt from my last experience and told him he was a genius and he let me help with the simple dishes. Soon the owners began to notice my cooking."

Blanc left after a year to work in Germany but before he could unpack he was called back to Oxford and made chef. For the next three years he worked 20 hours a day, cooking and reading, and saved £12,000 to open his own restaurant, the Quat' Saisons in Oxford, with his first wife, Jenny.

He has not looked back. He won a Michelin star within a year and after five years he fell in love with a small country house and rehoused the restaurant as Le Manoir aux Quat' Saisons, in Great Milton, near Oxford.

It now has two Michelin stars, 32 bedrooms and a cookery school.

In 1996 the first Petit Blanc opened its doors in Oxford and a second brasserie followed in Cheltenham in early 1998. There are plans to grow the Petit Blanc brand in other locations around the country.

Blanc wants to build a successful expanding enterprise but says success comes by looking beyond the bottom line: "If you lead by ideals rather than commercial thoughts, the bottom line will follow," he says. "Money puts the wrong light in people's eyes. It can be a negative energy."

> **'My father did not talk to me for two years and I wasn't allowed to come home because he thought I'd squandered my chances.'**

He says: "If you want to achieve something in life and you have a bit of talent you will succeed, but you have to want to. Entrepreneurs should never feel there are limits. I have never formally trained as a chef or a businessman. The key is to go beyond the barriers and reinvent yourself. I am a driven person. I like to create something beautiful because it is an irreversible process."

Towering ego put Bloomberg on path to top

**Original interview
25 May 1997**

Michael Bloomberg was ejected from Salomon after saying he could do things better. He now owns a $2 billion financial information empire.

Insecurity is not an emotion associated with Michael Bloomberg. He oozes self-confidence, as any smooth-talking American billionaire might. He insists most successful entrepreneurs must have some insecurity mixed with a "little bit" of ego to succeed, and ego is something more commonly associated with Bloomberg — the title of his book, Bloomberg by Bloomberg, makes the point.

His towering ego caused him to leave his job at Salomon Brothers and helped him make a success of his own company. In 15 years, he has created a $2 billion financial information company employing 4,500 people worldwide. His service has 105,000 subscribers, who receive asset prices, analysis and quotes on dedicated digital telephone lines.

Bloomberg was thrown off the Salomon Brothers trading floor in 1981 when he headed equity trading and sales, with a special responsibility for systems development. He had persisted in telling his bosses they were getting things wrong and that he could run the company better. "When I left, I had an idea to create a product to service Wall Street," says Bloomberg, who used the $10m he took out of the firm to found his company. "I had already invented some crude machines based on a computer program developed at Salomon. This simply offered stock and bond comparisons in terms of price and earnings, and I knew I could expand on it.

"I rented a one-room office and took three former Salomon staff with me. We split the work into data collection, software, hardware and selling. I'd have accepted a job with another bank, but none came along."

Things did not run smoothly for Bloomberg, who took charge of the selling side. "I spent three years trying to sell the system and went to every firm on the street [Wall Street]. They said: 'Great idea Mike. We're going to do it ourselves.' If the experience was easy, other people would have done it before. I found it humbling and I learned you've got to have confidence and the strength of your convictions, and once you start something, it's ego that keeps you going.

"It was a three-year process. The first year, you don't know any better. The third year you figure out there is light at the end of the tunnel rather than a train coming at you. The middle year is the most difficult."

Bloomberg made his breakthrough after being invited to a meeting at Merrill Lynch where he faced 30 lawyers, executives and accountants around a table. "I was on my own," he says. "Ed Moriarty, head of capital markets ran the meeting and asked Hank Alexander, their systems guy, to build a terminal using our ideas. Alexander said he could, but it would take him six months doing nothing else. I said I could do it quicker and Moriarty took out a contract for us to do it, much to the surprise of everyone else."

Bloomberg started small with his system, analysing a handful of securities, but he gradually expanded, establishing international offices and moving into television and radio. Merrill took the first 22 terminals and within two years had 1,000 and Bloomberg began making money in its third year. The securities house took a 30% stake and today it has 20% after a share buy-back.

Bloomberg says: "Entrepreneurs do too much. We picked something small and specific and grew it. Once you've got a product, you need to make it slightly better."

Bloomberg grew up in Medford, Massachusetts, where his father was a bookkeeper at a dairy. He studied engineering at The Johns Hopkins University in Baltimore, Maryland, and later went on to Harvard Business School.

He says he was not academically gifted and only really began to make the grade after he left college to work. He worked as a technician at a small electronics firm in the afternoons after his studies and earned further cash by cutting lawns and shovelling snow.

He joined Salomon, his first employer, after he graduated — and stayed for 15 years. He says the key to success is to work as a team: "You have to replace 'I' and 'me' with 'we' and 'us'. If you're selfish, you get a bigger piece of

> **'It was a three-year process. The first year, you don't know any better.'**

a smaller picture. Hard work and getting others to help you are important — in business people do favours for each other. Most people go out of their way for friends. I've never laid anyone off without agonising all night first," he claims. "I want to make sure if a member of staff gets hit by a truck, it hurts us — they should be missed, otherwise what were they doing here? But their loss should not be fatal to the company. We need to make sure there is backup."

Date of Birth
2 February 1942

Nationality
American

Present Company
Bloomberg LP

Age when first in business
Founded company in 1981, aged 39

Education
John Hopkins University; Harvard Business School

Early entrepreneurial ventures
Selling Christmas wreaths door-to-door for Boy Scouts

School holiday job
Parking cars and renting apartments

Qualifications
—

First job
In the "cage" at Salomon Brothers

Sales/Profit before tax 1997
Sales: $1.3 billion

Weeks holiday per year
Three weeks

Hobbies/Sports/Interests
Family, golf, planes, skiing

Idiosyncrasies, eg, car owned
Ford Expedition, Jeep

'I want to make sure if a member of staff gets hit by a truck, it hurts us — they should be missed, otherwise what were they doing here.'

Farmer's son says early bird gets the worm

Original interview
18 May 1997

The wealth of the Rothschilds spurred Andy Baker to overcome his Upstairs, Downstairs beginnings.

Andy Baker's company may revolve around people but his first business experience, at the age of 10, involved selling worms. Baker used to dig for ragworms on a beach near his home in Exbury, Hampshire. He controlled a team of six schoolmate diggers, selling 100 worms for 75p to fishermen as bait.

By the time he left school, he was making £150 a week, which funded the purchase of his first stereo. Baker still controls a team of young salesmen but with a different mission. He is founder chief executive of Glotel, one of Britain's fastest-growing private companies, which specialises in recruiting staff for information technology and accountancy through seven branded divisions, including Comms and PC People, Contract Accountants and Glotel Information Technology. It has expanded to 22 offices worldwide in eight years and 1998's results showed sales at £67.6m with operating profits of £1.8m.

The enterprise created a can of worms for Baker when he deliberately failed his 'A' levels so he would not be made to go to university but rather could pursue his business interests.

Generations of the Baker family grew up and worked at Exbury Gardens on the Rothschild estate — his father was an arable farmer, and his mother a cleaner — so while the family had little money, Baker was surrounded by great wealth.

"There was something that set off a trigger inside me about living in an environment where there was an obvious amount of wealth," he says. "I remember seeing all the cars and the money and knowing I could not get at it. It affected me and I knew I had to get off my backside and do something about it."

When his father lost his job because of arthritis, the family was deprived of its tied cottage and had to move to a different kind of estate, one run by a council. Baker decided that at the first opportunity, he would work for himself. "When dad lost his job and the house I remember thinking 'I'll have my own house, car and business'. That would be quite something — nobody had ever owned a house before in our

Date of Birth
16 July 1965

Nationality
British

Present Company
Glotel Plc

Age when first in business
24

Education
**10 'O' levels at comprehensive
school**

Early entrepreneurial ventures
**Bait digging for ragworms on
local beach**

School holiday job
**As above plus dishwasher at
local hotel**

Qualifications
—

First job
Clerical Assistant at DTI, London

Sales/Profit before tax 1997
(1998) Sales: £67.6m
(1998) Profit: £1.8m

Weeks holiday per year
Four weeks

Hobbies/Sports/Interests
Football (Fulham FC)

Idiosyncrasies, eg, car owned
—

'I love trying to inject
people with all the
skills needed to have
a great standard of
living, and I want it
to happen as quickly
as possible.'

family. I was always competitive at school, I had to be top."

Baker left school on a Friday and began work in London on the Monday as a clerk at the Department of Trade and Industry. "There was nothing to do and after a few months my manager encouraged me to look for other work. I went for an interview at Reed Employment, where my interviewer told me she had applied for a job at Hestair Computer Group, an IT recruitment company. It sounded right up my street, so I applied, too.

"I thought salesmen were flash so I went to Burtons and bought a glittering suit, which was later nicknamed by colleagues my disco suit. I knew I needed hard work, commitment and persistence, but I also knew I could do the job and told them that at the interview. They thought otherwise and showed me the door." But Baker did not take no for an answer. He called the company every day for three months and eventually won the Hestair people over after telling them he would be running the company within two years.

"They gave me a job with less money, but it was the time of the Big Bang and I made City contacts fast and became successful. Prior to my joining, the division turned over £200,000 and after 18 months we hit £2m. My manager left and I took over and began recruiting hungry, ambitious young people like myself."

Things started to go wrong when Baker's boss, Les Clark, left the company after disagreements with senior executives who wanted to become more involved with the division. Baker decided to leave as well and the two of them set up in business together. "We worked very long hours and absolutely attacked the market. I needed to feel good when I secured a deal so I would phone my old colleagues and other competitors to tell them."

He turned over more than £2m and made a profit of £100,000 in the first year, growing to sales of £4.8m by 1993 and employing eight staff. He opened his first office overseas in Amsterdam and then set up another in Atlanta. Baker's motivation seems to stem entirely from his childhood

> **'I remember seeing all the cars and the money and knowing I could not get at it.'**

experiences: "I love trying to inject people with all the skills needed to have a great standard of living, and I want it to happen as quickly as possible. I am totally driven by success and all the goodies that come with it. I can motivate and excite people.

"Success is down to hard work. There is a lot of pride in who makes it first to their desks in the mornings and I get tremendous pleasure from calling our competitors and hearing their voice-mail. Then I know they are still in bed and not making money."

Electronics firm sold client his own goods

Original interview
28 June 1998

Cliff Hardcastle could not resist profiting from another's mistake. His first big deal came when he bought parts from Thorn and sold them back at a hefty profit.

Big companies can sometimes be very stupid and such stupidity provides opportunities for entrepreneurs — particularly if they show a little enterprise.

Such was the experience of Cliff Hardcastle, founder–chairman of Densitron International, the electronic-components supplier, when he set up his first business in 1972. Within months of launching Perdix, an import-export operation, Hardcastle, an engineer-turned-salesman, was asked by the old Thorn EMI's defence division to supply digital displays. The buyer thought another part of Thorn, which had made displays, had ceased production and he needed an outside source. But Hardcastle discovered the buyer was mistaken — the Thorn plant had simply relocated to the West Country.

So Hardcastle headed west, obtained a quote for the product, added 30% to the price and went back to his customer, who then placed a big order. Thus did Hardcastle sell Thorn its own products.

But chutzpah alone cannot a company make. Hardcastle knew how to exploit more conventional business opportunities. At about the time of the Thorn order, Dennis Taylor, a former colleague, asked him for advice on hi-fi speakers he had seen in Hungary. Hardcastle wrote to the Hungarian embassy on the pretext that he wanted to import the speakers and asked for samples, which he planned to pass to Taylor.

But the plan backfired when he was called into the embassy to be confronted by 18 staff from the state-run company and their Communist advisers. They had flown in to tie up what they hoped would be a big deal. He found the speakers were good quality and, at £6 a pair, good value. He knew nothing about consumer marketing but he spotted an opportunity.

Instead of ordering samples, he offered to buy 600. But the Hungarians thought this was too small an order. He then said he meant 600 pairs but they were still not impressed. Only when he said he meant 600 pairs of each model they made was a deal done.

Taylor invested £3,000 on stock and rent on a small office at Chislehurst,

Kent, which was crammed with speakers. Initially sales were poor but then the speakers were reviewed favourably in a magazine, and within three days Perdix had run out of stock. Hardcastle says: "Running out was the cleverest thing we did because it whipped up demand. Shops took advance orders and we were selling 4,000 speakers a month. It gave us spare capital to develop the business."

Spare capital was something he needed. Perdix was set up with £3,000 of savings when Hardcastle became disillusioned working for others. He was an electronics engineer for 10 years but shifted to sales because he thought that was the way to get to the top in business.

He started Perdix after falling out with the boss of Guest International, a Yugoslav firm. He says: "I had always thought of running my own business and had set about finding out how businesses were run. I was a long way from the decision-making process and felt frustrated — progression within a large company can be slow. I wanted to understand why decisions were made and play some part in them. I have always had a desire for power and authority."

He thought he had enough skills, having learnt the basics of importing and having become aware of good products not made in Britain. His niche was items with novel features that needed technical skills to sell them. Hardcastle began working from home and searched for products and clients. He says: "I had no ambition other than to make a living. I did not know anything

about book-keeping, I just looked at the bank balance and knew what margin I needed to pay my way."

After five years the speaker business was sold to Richer Sounds for £50,000, and Hardcastle concentrated on importing industrial electronics. By 1983 his business, Densitron, was making £100,000 on sales of £1.5m. Three years later when it floated, profits had grown to £1m and sales to £10m.

Most recent figures show 1997 profits at £1.7m on sales of £28m, including exports to America, Australia and Japan. The bulk of those sales come from a factory at Biggin Hill, Kent. Staff numbers total 400.

> **'I had always thought of running my own business and had set about finding out how businesses were run.'**

Hardcastle, the son of a naval gunner and a domestic help, went to Addey & Stanhope grammar school in Deptford, south London. As a child he wanted to be a bacteriologist but he became interested in electronics during national service and, at 20, took his first job with Philips. He says a photographic memory, curiosity and flexibility have been the keys to his success, not workaholism. "I have never worked more than a 60-hour week," he says. "I don't believe in working long hours. Hard work on a useless project still renders it a useless project."

Date of Birth
24 August 1934

Nationality
English

Present Company
Denistron International Plc

Age when first in business
38

Education
Grammar School 'A' level Physics, Chemistry, Maths. RAF (Electronics). Technical College HNC (Applied Physics)

Early entrepreneurial ventures
Processing roll films for chemists and taking pictures

School holiday job
As above

Qualifications
HNC (Applied Physics)

First job
Technical Assistant, Mullard Radio Valve Co Ltd (Phillips subsidiary)

Sales/Profit before tax 1997
Sales: £28m Profit: £1.7m

Weeks holiday per year
Four weeks

Hobbies/Sports/Interests
Football, cricket, golf, badminton, photography, organ-playing

Idiosyncrasies, eg, car owned
Time

'I don't believe in working long hours. Hard work on a useless project still renders it a useless project.'

My Brilliant Idea

Mike Gooley
travel

Katharine Hamnett
fashion

Tony Mack
air charters

Virginia Lopalco
food

Masaya Nakamura
electronic arcades

Dawna Walter
storage products

Escape from army led to Trailfinders

**Original interview
20 July 1997**

Kicking against the regimentation of boarding school and army life led Mike Gooley to found his go-it-alone holiday enterprise.

After four unhappy years at prep school, then a "reasonably happy" spell at public school, and 12 good years in the army, Mike Gooley was desperate to take charge of his life and start his own business. It must have seemed a big gamble but it has paid off.

Today Gooley is chairman of Trailfinders, the specialist travel agent with a reputation for being the operator most self-respecting adventurers use. It steers away from package holidays, specialising in discounted long-haul flights and selling tailor-made trips through its eleven branches.

1997 was its most successful year so far, with sales of £262m and profits of £6.5m (after charitable donations of £1.35m). It employs 711 staff, mostly graduates who are experienced travellers. The skills Gooley picked up with the SAS in Malaya, Oman, Borneo and Aden and his hunger to do his own thing lie behind his approach to entrepreneurialism.

"I spent my life being told to go here, there and everywhere," he says. "I fast realised there was another way of living. The army nurtured a herd ethic from which I wanted to escape. I felt there were better ways of doing things and I was attracted to the idea of being my own boss and being allowed to make mistakes."

His first business venture, a gold and diamond prospecting business in Guyana, was definitely a mistake. He and five army mates clubbed together £2,000 and headed for the jungle. But once there, they realised they had upset an 'agreement' between the locals and the government and they were 'encouraged' to return to England.

Gooley then turned his hand to hawking cosmetics as part of a network-selling organisation. He picked up the basic principles of selling: "People buy for fear of loss or hope of gain," he says — but once again the business came to nothing. But with Trailfinders it was third time lucky. He became interested in the overland tours that were fashionable in the late 1960s. Land Rovers used to set off for Kathmandu ill-equipped for the journey and offering few guarantees for the paying passengers.

Date of Birth
13 October 1936

Nationality
British

Present Company
Trailfinders Ltd

Age when first in business
31

Education
St Johns, Beaumont; St George College, Weybridge; Royal Military Academy, Sandhurst

Early entrepreneurial ventures
—

School holiday job
Whatever I could find for as long as the holiday

Qualifications
—

First job
—

Sales/Profit before tax 1997
—

Weeks holiday per year
Event-driven; three to six weeks

Hobbies/Sports/Interests
—

Idiosyncrasies, eg, car owned
Aston Martin

'I have always had a flair for organisation and have taken all the positive things from the army and applied them to Trailfinders.'

Gooley says: "We thought about setting up our own tour, but when we explored the opportunities we realised the market was flooded. What we did was spot a niche for an agent to take bookings for these tours and become a broker.

"Three former army friends once again put together £1,000, and we started advertising and created some brochures. We set about representing the tours, weeding out the cowboys as much as we could, and we opened our first shop in London's Earls Court Road."

It took seven years to make a profit. The business finally took off in the late 1980s when Gooley pieced together various long-haul flights from different airlines, which found certain routes hard to sell. He packaged them together as heavily discounted round-the-world tickets for travellers wanting lots of stop-offs on year-long trips. He earned a reputation as a reliable value-for-money operator and is now the market leader in his sector.

Gooley says risk-taking is part of his nature: "I was in the SAS so I have always lived with an element of risk — it is just a matter of evaluating the odds. I built up physical and mental stamina, and learnt how to use my initiative.

"I have relied on my wits for most of my life, I was placed in a Jesuit boarding school from the age of eight. If you can survive four years at St Johns, there is little you can't go on to do. It was like a prisoner of war camp."

Gooley is the son of an Irish Guards warrant officer, but his mother, a nurse, was the main breadwinner, building up a successful nursing-home business. But she died when Gooley was 15 and the business collapsed. "I saw how hard it was to build the business and how quickly it slipped away," he says. "This made me even more cautious when growing Trailfinders." He supplemented the family income in the holidays by working as a hod carrier. He was also a joiner's mate before joining the army.

Gooley is driven by fear of failure. "I was brought up in a highly competitive environment," he says. "My phobia and terror is of failing. The greater you succeed, the greater the scope for fail-

> **'I was attracted to the idea of being my own boss and being allowed to make mistakes.'**

ure. The difference between success and failure is only a matter of degrees."

Of his success he says: "I have always had a flair for organisation and have taken all the positive things from the army and applied them to Trailfinders. Success has been a bit like rolling a stone up a hill with a pack on your back. You come across a lot of false peaks, but when you really get to the top the bloody thing starts rolling down the other side and there's no stopping it!"

Hamnett seeks hide after a fashion

**Original interview
6 December 1998**

Turning problems into opportunities is a mark of a successful entrepreneur. That much is true of Katharine Hamnett, the fashion designer, whose eponymous clothing business was the product more of accident than deliberation.

Hamnett's first stab at business came when she created Tuttabankem with a partner, but she threw in the towel after five years because it was going nowhere — she preferred to work as a freelance designer producing international collections for fashion houses. Although ambitious, she had little idea then that she might eventually create a fashion brand with sales of £100m.

But a problem with a client in 1978 spurred her to abandon freelancing once again for serious business. She had spent three months designing a collection for Gudle, a French company with 60 stores, when it went bust leaving her short £17,000 in unpaid design fees. She had to think of an idea, and quickly, to replace the income that would have flowed had the designs gone into production. She came up with the idea of making some of the designs in leather instead of cheaper fabrics and — for the first time — put her own name on the label.

Thus the Katharine Hamnett brand was born. "I knew I would not be able to recoup the cost on volume and had to find an alternative way to boost the return on each item I made" she says. "That way I was able to make much larger margins because people were prepared to pay higher prices for quality material." She borrowed £500 from a friend, Mark Young, created some prototype garments and approached the top stores in Britain and in Italy and France. They included Joseph, which went on to be a big customer.

The stores had taken some of her designs in the past and were willing to give her a break and it paid off in style for both designer and retailer.

Hamnett soon switched into cotton and silk, quickly creating a recognised look, and she backed up her design with an unusual sales technique: "I did it the French way. I took a stand at various trade shows and instead of inviting key buyers and distributors I whipped up a lot of interest and hype by being really snotty, and taking the approach of vetting people to see if

61

they were good enough to come in. People got very wound up and were so grateful when I let them in because they had met the so-called criteria. It tainted their judgement in my favour."

Instead of splashing out on expensive display materials, she would wait until the other exhibitors had finished their stands and would then raid their rubbish for castoffs. "It was pretty outrageous what they would chuck out," she says.

Sales took off enabling her to move within two years to a small factory on an industrial estate in London's Islington, and to employ 15 people. Originally the plan was to make her clothes in Britain but a series of burglaries caused her to think again and she decided to outsource manufacturing to Italy.

In 1981 she diversified into menswear and soon after that she began to export, gaining her first licence in Japan in 1984. Today she has about 40 Japanese concessions and 17 licencees. In 1986 Hamnett opened her first London store and four years later she was employing 25 people, mostly designers. She now has stores in Hong Kong, Taiwan, and Korea, having recently moved into fashion sportswear and jeans.

Companies House figures for her British businesses show Katharine Hamnett Limited with losses of £184,344 in 1997 on sales of £1.9m. Katharine Hamnett Designs made a £310,115 profit on £2.4m of sales while Katharine Hamnett Retail made

a £18,282 profit on £774,443 of sales. Hamnett grew up near Tunbridge Wells, Kent, but she travelled around the world with her family because her father was an RAF defence attaché. Educated at Cheltenham Ladies College she developed her trading skills early, designing dolls and persuading her parents' friends to buy them for £5 each. She hated boarding school but was moderately academic and went on to study at St Martins School of Art.

She describes her qualities as "stubbornness, being bolshy, speaking French, tenacity, working hard and being able to put your foot down."

> **'I was able to make much larger margins because people would pay more for quality material.'**

"I'm an autocrat," she says. "People tend to do what I like and then shit themselves until the result comes good. If I was not working for myself I would be unemployable. I do believe it is better to make your own mistakes and suffer from them than live in ignorance. I think it's very interesting being me."

Name: **Katharine Hamnett**

Date of Birth
Some time in the distant past

Nationality
British

Present Company
Katharine Hamnett

Age when first in business
19

Education
**7 'O' levels, 3 'A' levels.
Cheltenham Ladies College;
St Martins College of Art, London**

Early entrepreneurial ventures
**Made dolls, aged 14, and sold to
parents' friends**

School holiday job
—

Qualifications
**Diploma in Art & Design.
Professor of Fashion & Textiles,
London Institute**

First job
**Pretended to be freelance fashion
designer while still at college**

Sales/Profit before tax 1997
See text

Weeks holiday per year
Ten plus weeks

Hobbies/Sports/Interests
**Archaeology, walking, partying,
travelling, art, photography**

Idiosyncrasies, eg, car owned
**Austin A30 1956, a small boat —
my favourite things. One home in
London and one in Majorca**

Flying start for charter chief

Original interview
20 April 1997

Tony Mack, chairman of Air London International, created a thriving charter business by finding a way to earn money from unused aircraft at his father's flying school.

Tony Mack was introduced to aircraft at an early age. He was born in a Nissen hut at Bournemouth's Hurn airport — a late arrival who made an emergency landing on a groundsheet.

Everything pointed to a career in aviation and in adult life he has made his name transforming his father's flying school into what he claims is the world's top corporate-jet charter business. Air London floated on the Unlisted Securities Market (USM) in 1989 and moved up to a full listing in 1995. In 1998 it turned over £50m and has a market value of £30m.

Mack joined Airways Training, his father's business, as a teaboy aged 21. It owned six twin-engined Beagles and Pipers, which were used to train former airforce pilots for their commercial licences. The aircraft spent much of their time on the ground due to rules restricting the number of hours a pilot could fly. Mack's duties ranged from cleaning the aircraft and sorting charts and flight plans to updating the books.

His first break came after he realised the time the aeroplanes spent on the ground was wasted revenue, and he tried to find ways to maximise their use. "We began to rent out the aircraft at weekends," he says. "We used the name Air London because passengers were put off flying in aircraft supplied by Airways Training — it sounded like we weren't qualified. The charter was just a sideline, with the core business still in teaching."

But Mack made this sideline into a multi-million pound business that superseded Airways Training. The chartering took off and Mack found he was turning away customers because he did not have the capacity or flexibility.

But then he realised he did not need to own the planes to run an airline, and thus formed the basis of the business: broking charter flights. "I realised there was a market there for someone to act as a broker between people who own aircraft, which spend much of their life on the tarmac not earning money, and companies desperate to get staff across the world at a moment's notice.

Date of Birth
10 December 1948

Nationality
English

Present Company
Air London International Plc

Age when first in business
21

Education
**Imberhorne Secondary; Crawley
Technical College**

Early entrepreneurial ventures
—

School holiday job
**Ace Freighters (went bust);
Aviation Instruments, Turners Air
Agency**

Qualifications
**Private Pilot's Licence;
Administrative Accountant**

First job
Coutts & Co (Bankers)

Sales/Profit before tax 1997
Sales: £42m Profit: £2.3m

Weeks holiday per year
Eight weeks since relinquished MD

Hobbies/Sports/Interests
**Sailing (owns racing yacht *McFly*),
squash, skiing, horse riding and
playing golf (badly)**

Idiosyncrasies, eg, car owned
Ferrari 355, BMW 740

**'Entrepreneurs
should just go out
and do it —
it is easier to get
forgiveness than
permission.'**

"We did not need to be limited by the number of planes we owned. We could use other people's. It was just a matter of putting the two together. I had a vision of creating a smart brokers' room, like a City trading floor. We would benefit from economies of scale through the number of planes we chartered, but the most difficult thing was convincing my father to sell all our aircraft. Dad thought it was a ploy so I wouldn't have to clean them. He believed you needed to own aircraft to run an airline and be a 'real' player."

Mack managed to win over his father and opened a small office in Gatwick next to a waste outlet. He accelerated his dream of running a smart broking office by producing a glossy brochure with pictures of a major airline's office — he did not claim it was his office but let customers assume so.

"The scheme almost backfired when a client came over from France and turned up at our small office," says Mack. "He asked to be taken to the main trading floor. When I explained this was it, he was so impressed with my initiative that he is still one of my best clients."

The business expanded rapidly, taking £1m in 1980 and £5m by 1987. It currently employs 70 people in high-tech offices in Crawley, France and Germany with a 12% marketshare.

Recent clients include showbusiness stars such as Eddie Murphy, Pierce Brosnan, Gloria Estefan and Sharon Stone as well as politicians and royalty. Air London is just as capable of scrambling a Lear jet as a Jumbo to transport an entire salesforce to a conference.

Mack grew up travelling from one airfield to another. He worked part-time at Gatwick Airport during his school holidays and his first full-time job was with Coutts Bank because "that's where all the money was." But he got bored and after two years left to join his father. "Everyone kept marrying within the bank, and every new idea I came up with was met with 'We tried that in 1802'."

Mack says the key to success is being good with people, both staff and customers. "I am good at selecting and motivating our team," he says. "We

> **'We did not need to be limited by the number of planes we owned. We could use other people's.'**

don't just satisfy our customers — they never thank you if you give them what they expect — we try to delight them."

He says the best way to avoid pitfalls when starting in business is to learn from someone who has done it. "It is all very well learning from a sailing coach, but it's the world champion who will give the best tips. Entrepreneurs should just go out and do it — it is easier to get forgiveness than permission," he says. "Perseverance is important at the beginning, then attitude after that. You are either in business to win or not; there is no in-between."

Knight rescues pasta damsel in distress

**Original interview
15 June 1997**

A stranger's generosity saved a struggling restaurateur who went on to found Pasta Reale, the £16m pasta maker.

There are few entrepreneurs who have trodden quite such a rocky road to the top as Virginia Lopalco. Her rags-to-riches story reads more like a Hollywood screenplay than a business success story.

An Italian peasant girl desperate to make something of her life flees to England and opens a restaurant. But her world collapses when the business she has slaved to build is literally torn apart. Facing bankruptcy, she throws herself at the mercy of a stranger, who bails her out, setting her on the road to riches. She ends up making millions and later bails him out.

Lopalco built Pasta Reale from scratch, with no training, and her success is proof that hard work and determination — and some luck — are the ingredients for a thriving business. She and her husband, Salvatore, together with Roberto Santi, her brother, spent years saving enough money to buy their own restaurant and found a transport cafe in Croydon, Surrey. To boost the day's takings they started opening

in the evenings serving Italian food. As the night trade began to dominate the business they hired builders to convert the cafe into a proper restaurant — Bella Venezia.

"We gave the builders all the money we had," she says. "They knocked out the windows and the front wall but they went bust the next day and never came back. It was mid-October — a few loyal customers braved the freezing weather but the novelty soon wore off and we were left with half a restaurant, no customers and no money. I tried everywhere, the bank and friends to see if they could help. I was at my wits end when a carpet salesman walked through what was left of the door and I told him the story. He must have seen the desperation in my eyes. He wrote me a cheque for £2,000 with no provisos and it was this charitable, out-of-the-blue act that made all the difference. This time I did not pay the builders until they finished the work and within two years had paid the good Samaritan back."

Like many successful businesses Pasta Reale started as a sideline: Lopalco used to make fresh pasta for the diners, and would take the excess to a local delicatessen on a sale-or-return basis. "The delicatessen would sell out regularly and the idea formed in my head that we could do it commercially. I went to the library and noted all the delicatessens in London, found out what they sold and whether they would be interested in our pasta. We decided to start small and it took a year to find the right premises, a disused bakery in Balcombe, Sussex."

In 1967 Lopalco formed a partnership with her husband and Santi. The first products took a while to perfect, but once the teething problems were solved, she was soon selling to Harrods, Fortnum & Mason, and Waitrose.

In its first year, Pasta Reale made £500 on sales of £78,000, and in 1983 it moved to bigger premises and started supplying a supermarket chain. It opened a £12m factory in 1992, and in 1993 made its first million pounds profit on sales of £6m. In 1997 it made £3m on sales of £20m and now employs 110 people having become brand leader in a flourishing market.

Lopalco was born in a small village in the northern Italian province of Treviso to tenant farmers, but her father travelled to Belgium to work as a miner to supplement the family's meagre income. Her mother brought in more money by working 12-hour shifts in a textile mill, leaving Lopalco to raise her brothers and sisters. "I was the eldest girl and had to look after the family," she says. "I was seven and had to make the beds and used a chair to reach the washing-up. I was good at school but at age 11 it became too expensive and I went into service working as a maid in people's homes. When I could, I used to borrow my brothers' books and hide in fields to educate myself."

Lopalco convinced her mother she had to go abroad, first to France and then to England as an au pair. To earn extra cash she worked as a waitress at Trattoria d'Otello in London's Dean Street, where at 20 she met her future husband, then a chef.

She began to think about owning her own restaurant but fell pregnant. "You have to make your mind up in business and follow it at whatever cost. It was heartbreaking but I sent my two young children home to my mother so I could

> **'The delicatessen would sell out regularly and the idea formed in my head that we could do it commercially.'**

earn enough money to start a restaurant. If you don't do it when you've got the energy, you'll never do it. I wasn't going to bring children into the world to live the life I went through.

"I wanted to fight to create something better. The harder I worked the faster I'd get my children back. There were some low times but you have to pick yourself up if you stumble."

Surprisingly, her favourite dish is English. "I have to taste a lot of pasta," she says, "but at the end of the day nothing beats a traditional roast beef."

Name: Virginia Lopalco

Date of Birth
7 March 1940

Nationality
Italian

Present Company
Pasta Reale Ltd

Age when first in business
27

Education
Elementary schooling. My real education was experiencing real life situations. I worked as a nanny, a translator, a washer-up and waitress and a home help. That's how I learnt about people and what it takes to succeed

Early entrepreneurial ventures
Opened a transport cafe and changed it into a restaurant. Established a catering and restaurant business. Developed a small factory, then another, and then another

School holiday job
Worked on the farm in a kitchen and assisted my mother as a cleaner — all unpaid

Qualifications
See Education

First job
—

Sales/Profit before tax 1997
Turnover: £20m

Weeks holiday per year
More now, but holidays were a day here and there, even when the children were very young

Hobbies/Sports/Interests
—

Idiosyncrasies, eg, car owned
Curtain-making, gardening and spending time with my husband. These have never been 'normal' for us — the only constant normal for us was hard work

'You have to make your mind up in business . . . if you don't do it when you've got the energy, you'll never do it.'

Pac-Man creator bites into County Hall

Original interview
31 August 1997

Namco's Masaya Nakamura built a global entertainment empire, including a new venture in London, County Hall.

Many of the world's most successful entrepreneurs have begun their business careers in extremely modest circumstances. Masaya Nakamura started out working for his father on the top floor of a department store in Yokohama repairing air guns. But to survive, the business had to diversify. So Nakamura attached a piece of cork to some string and created a child's pop-gun. It was an instant success and he began to make contacts in the toy world.

He went on to buy two coin-operated rocking-horse rides and set them up in the department store to entertain children while their parents went shopping. Forty years on, Namco, the company which Nakamura started, has grown into a £1 billion multinational listed on the Tokyo stock exchange.

The business took off in the 1970s when it moved into arcade games and created Pac-Man, one of the first computer games to sweep the world. Namco bought the Japanese arm of Atari, the computer-games console company, and now has computer hardware and software divisions, a film-production business, a restaurant chain and indoor and outdoor theme parks.

Namco made profits of £46.5m on sales of £746m in 1997. In August 1997 it unveiled its latest venture, Namco Station, an indoor computer-games arcade with electronic bowling alleys, skiing, and rally-driving set up at London's County Hall, once the headquarters of the Greater London Council.

Back in 1955 Nakamura could never have imagined such leisure pursuits as he worked at the Matsuya department store.

Masaya Nakamura had studied ship-building at Yokohama National University. But Japan's economic situation at that time meant it could not afford to build ships and there were few job opportunities in the industry. So instead he helped his father with his gun business.

"I would do everything from sweeping the floor to designing posters advertising the workshop," says Nakamura. "I would spend my evenings cycling

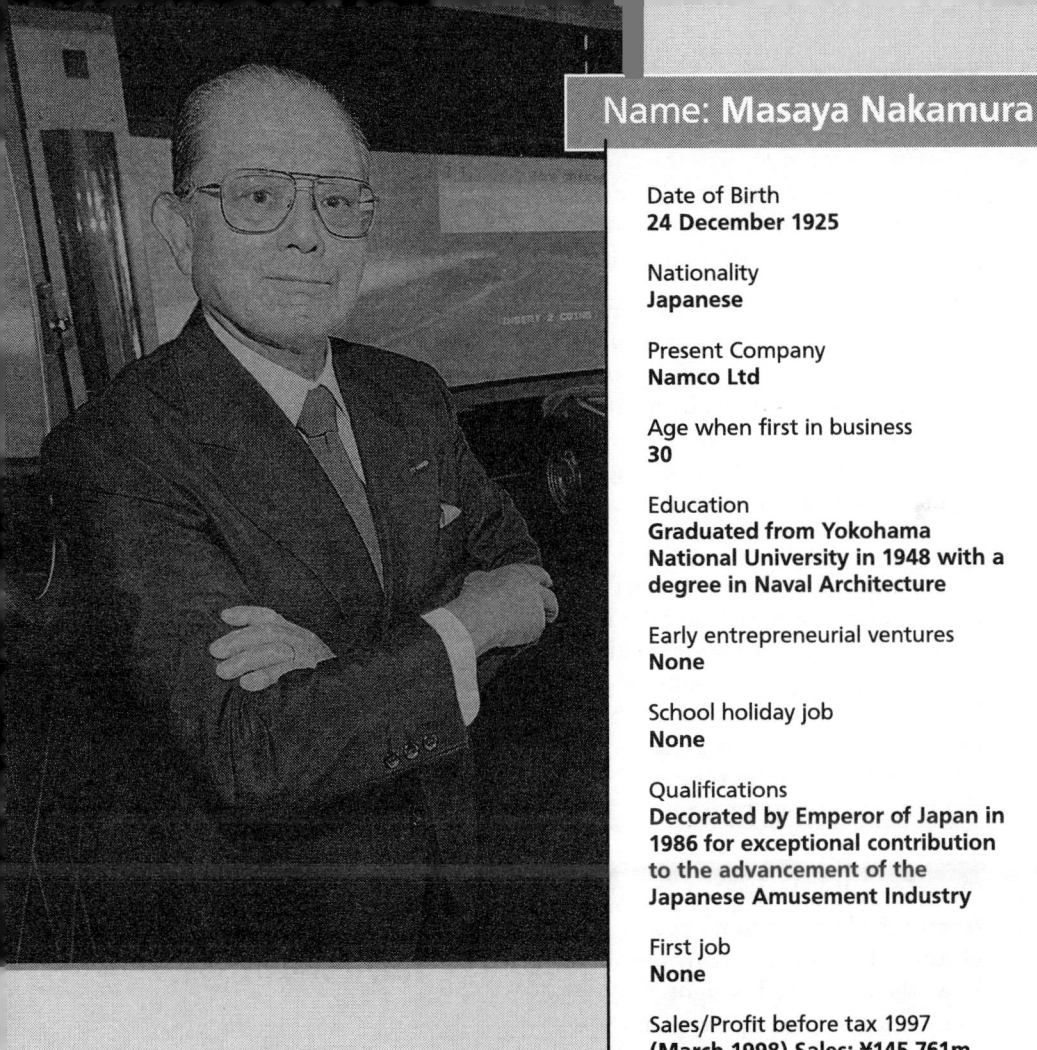

Date of Birth
24 December 1925

Nationality
Japanese

Present Company
Namco Ltd

Age when first in business
30

Education
Graduated from Yokohama National University in 1948 with a degree in Naval Architecture

Early entrepreneurial ventures
None

School holiday job
None

Qualifications
Decorated by Emperor of Japan in 1986 for exceptional contribution to the advancement of the Japanese Amusement Industry

First job
None

Sales/Profit before tax 1997
(March 1998) Sales: ¥145,761m
(March 1998) Profit: ¥9,075m

Weeks holiday per year
123 days

Hobbies/Sports/Interests
Golf, the play of 'go'

Idiosyncrasies, eg, car owned
None

'If you devote yourself to a principle in life, no matter how much effort it takes to achieve it, it will not be painful.'

around Tokyo pasting up the posters. We were eventually able to sell new air guns, and I would visit the suppliers."

But he was prompted to move into children's toys by a series of regulations that threatened to ruin the rifle business. First, the Japanese government moved to restrict firearms ownership in general. It then introduced tighter regulations over which birds people were allowed to shoot.

Nakamura said: "There was a reduction in the amount of repairs and the number of sales, and I hit upon this idea where we could sell the guns, with a little adaptation, as harmless toys. We were able to make a living from it, and this set me thinking about how to amuse children.

"In most other department stores they had children's playgrounds, but not at Matsuya — I saw the future and bought some rides which I operated at the top of the store."

His father retired and the gun business faded away. But Nakamura moved into a second department store, Mitsukoshi, and expanded the amusements with a 3D sound and picture machine, and a pond where children could scoop goldfish and take them home.

Nakamura employed three staff and would still clean and oil the rides himself. The company expanded to operate 10 play areas in various department stores across Japan, and in 1966 it started building its own attractions when manufacturers could not keep up with demand.

"Manufacturers tried to muscle in to operate their own play areas," says Nakamura. "So we had to be innovative. We were the first company to approach Disney for licences to use their characters on rides. Bambi and Dumbo drew a lot of attention and added value."

In 1974 Namco bought Atari (Japan) and moved into the electronic-arcade market. By 1982 it was making £40m and employing 200 staff. It floated on the Tokyo stock exchange in 1988 and four years later opened its first outdoor theme park in Tokyo. Today it has 1,000 indoor theme parks.

> **'I hit upon this idea where we could sell the air guns, with a little adaptation, as harmless toys.'**

Nakamura is philosophical about his success. He believes in a Japanese proverb that says if you really enjoy your work everything else follows. "It is all to do with attitude," he says. "An employee must enjoy his work; it is not enough that he wants to enjoy it. If you devote yourself to a principle in life, no matter how much effort it takes to achieve it, it will not be painful.

Confucius wrote, 'To be fond of knowledge is better than simply acquiring it, and to take delight in it is far better than simply being fond of it'."

Wardrobe organiser makes a tidy profit

Original interview 22 June 1997

Dawna Walter went into business when she saw scope for bringing order to our cluttered lives.

Dawna Walter started The Holding Company, which sells storage and organisation products, after an abortive search for a shop that could supply a system for storing items in her wardrobe.

Walter moved to London from America in 1992 to marry an English lawyer and started to redecorate their mews house when she realised there were no firms specialising in 'closet organisers'.

Knowing the American market was big, she decided to get in first over here and opened her first shop on the King's Road, London in April 1995. Since then the business has grown with sales hitting £1.3m in 1996. In that same year Walter raised £750,000 on Ofex to fund expansion. She now has a mail-order catalogue and plans to open stores in Dartford, Kent and Newcastle in 1999.

Walter began her working life as a teacher, tried her hand as a political fundraiser and then moved into marketing. Her experience in organising political campaigns taught her to be meticulous and prompted her to build a company around improving home and office organisation.

As Dawna Rosenberg, she graduated from the University of Massachusetts in 1974 and became a nursery teacher. "That's what girls did," she says, "teaching or nursing. There weren't very many other choices." She left teaching because it was not stimulating and went into retailing.

A friend of a friend asked her if she would join the Carrington Williams congressional campaign in Richmond, Virginia, in 1976.

"I spent seven months scheduling his wife, and organising events — even writing speeches. He lost, but I got asked to do the same thing for a senate campaign in Illinois. It was a dirty campaign and controversial. It was essential to have an eye for detail while organising a strategy of appearances for the candidate. It was a matter of co-ordinating the media, the police and a host of venues. Jimmy Carter, Ted Kennedy and Muhammad Ali all paid visits."

Walter says that after a year she had been exposed to the workings of the political system and had access to good

73

contacts. "I found you have a finite time to organise things, and if they do not run like clockwork it meant the difference between winning or losing. You can apply the same principle to business.

"We would work to 23-minute schedules of S&M (shake and mingle), and I had to be organised and resourceful. This helps me with sourcing now. I co-ordinated all the appearances from dealing with the flowers, tasting the food and reading the road maps to making conversation with the president."

Walter made such an impression she ended up at the White House as part of a fundraising team. When President Carter lost the election in 1980, Walter moved to New York and worked for a charity, but was soon recruited as a shopping mall marketing director.

"It wasn't as big a career change as it seems," she says. "I was interviewed by a woman who had also worked on some political campaigns and with my previous retail experience she felt I had the ideal skills. I loved the job and looked after some 200 stores."

Walter spent the next 10 years working in various malls until the bottom fell out of the market. She came over to London after meeting Jerry Walter, an English solicitor whom she married, and on realising there was a huge gap in the storage-products market, she decided to fill it.

"I just needed the start-up cash," she says. "I approached one of my husband's clients, Michael Sinclair (a businessman), and started a presentation with mood boards and market statistics, but after 10 minutes he had already committed £250,000, which I matched with £100,000 and we opened The Holding Company nine months later."

Dawna Walter says of her success: "I'm an organised person and can do 15 things at one time and keep track. I am direct and I don't put up with bad service.

> **'I found you have a finite time to organise things, and if they do not run like clockwork it meant the difference between winning or losing.'**

"Being an American in England helps and I have self-confidence in what I do. People tend to look on the downside in business — I see a cup half-full while people over here see it as half-empty. Attitude makes a difference."

Date of Birth
3 April 1952

Nationality
USA/British

Present Company
The Holding Company

Age when first in business
Own business, aged 42

Education
**BA (Urban Education), University
of Massachusetts, Amherst, 1974**

Early entrepreneurial ventures
**Embroidered bell-bottom jeans at
University to make pocket money**

School holiday job
Summer camp counsellor

Qualifications
BA (Urban Education)

First job
**Stocking girl for ladies clothing
shop at 13**

Sales/Profit before tax 1997
—

Weeks holiday per year
One week taken, four weeks given

Hobbies/Sports/Interests
**Knitwear design, interior design,
product design, and poodles**

Idiosyncrasies, eg, car owned
—

'I'm an organised
person and can do 15
things at one time
and keep track.
I am direct and I
don't put up with
bad service.'

Good Connections

David Richards
motorsport engineering

Frank Cohen
home improvement

April Ducksbury
model agency

Patrick McGovern
i.t. publishing

Janet Reger
lingerie

Adrian Reynard
motorsports

Former rally champion finds winning formula

Original interview
12 July 1998

David Richards has combined the racing driver's love of risks with the accountant's natural caution to create a successful business empire.

Making the most of contacts and exploiting a good reputation are often critical to success in a young business.

This was the case for David Richards, founder of Prodrive, the engineering company involved in motor racing, mainstream passenger car engineering and automotive component supply. Prodrive was a finalist in The Sunday Times/NatWest Business Enterprise Awards in 1998, and Richards was at the British Grand Prix in the same year as chief executive of Benetton Formula, the Formula One racing team.

Richards took a job driving for the British Leyland (BL) factory racing team in 1976 but found he had a lot of time on his hands in between races. He always wanted to run his own business and believed there was a gap in the motor-racing market between business-men who did not understand the sport and racing drivers who lacked commer-cial accumen. He felt he could fill this niche, exploiting his skill at the wheel and his accountancy background.

Richards had no launch capital and decided he had to start as a consultant. He contacted the sponsors, manufac-turers and team owners he knew to convince them of his merits and even-tually the schmoozing paid off when he landed a contract with Rothmans. He says: "I had built up a good name and reputation. I knew someone at Rothmans and knew it was looking to establish some promotional activity in Bahrain and Oman, so I put in a bid to set up a Middle East championship.

"I spent my time travelling to each country and telling police chiefs what we wanted to do. I then had to find marshals to run the race and in many cases establish local motor clubs. They were trying days and taught me a lot about diplomacy and perseverance." Richards' commercial career ran for some time in tandem with his compe-tition ambitions. But he eventually left BL to concentrate on his business and took on three staff. Originally it was not much more than a hobby, but his ambition grew and he put his business into a company that he called David Richards Autosports.

He got his second contract when his contacts with Fiat came good, enabling

Date of Birth
3 June 1952

Nationality
British

Present Company
Prodrive Ltd

Age when first in business
24

Education
Brynhyfryd School, Ruthin

Early entrepreneurial ventures
Photographer, tour guide

School holiday job
—

Qualifications
—

First job
**Freelance marketing consultant
to Rothmans**

Sales/Profit before tax 1997
Sales: £42.2m Profit: £2.7m

Weeks holiday per year
Four weeks

Hobbies/Sports/Interests
**Helicopter pilot, tennis, classic
sports cars**

Idiosyncrasies, eg, car owned
**Owner of a number of
contemporary and classic
Aston Martins**

'I have a strange
mix of skills.
Accountancy has
taught me to be
prudent and racing
is all about taking
things to the limit.'

him to set up its first rally team in Britain. He says: "I just knew a lot of people and could take the problem of setting up Fiat's team away from them. But it was not big money and in the early days our existence was very much hand to mouth."

From there Richards expanded. He won £100,000 of sponsorship so that he could start racing again and he acted as an agent, representing tyre and oil companies in the British motor-racing world.

In 1981 he formed a design company to do creative work for sponsors and formed a clothing and merchandising business. In 1984 he started his own team but the business only really accelerated in 1987.

Richards was still just breaking even on sales of £2m and after losing a big Rothmans contract — because changes to regulations made it less attractive for sponsors — he decided to restructure the company. He borrowed £2m from Swiss Bank Corporation and set up an engineering division to service his own team and the others he was running. He then renamed the company Prodrive.

"I realised engineering was common to everything we did and I thought how inefficient it was for each team to have its own engineering staff. We centralised it and hired it out to other clients."

The Banbury-based company moved into profit in 1992 and by 1993 it was making £350,000 on sales of £24m. Since then profits surged to reach

£2.7m in 1997 on sales of £42.2m. Employing 360 people, it has three divisions: engineering design for motorsport and road cars; sales and marketing; and the motorsports division, which manages teams.

Richards now plans to develop Prodrive as a brand and is considering merging aspects of the company with a partner. Last year he held talks with Benetton, to buy its formula one team, which he runs, but they came to nothing.

Richards grew up on a farm in Ruthin, Clwyd, and went to Brynhyfryd Comprehensive. After school, he studied accountancy with Cook & Co, a Liverpool firm, but was

> **'I just knew a lot of people and could take the problem of setting up Fiat's team away from them.'**

more interested in racing motorbikes and then cars on the farm track. His love of racing rally cars led to his BL job. He won the national rally championships in 1975 and the world championships in 1981.

He says his grounding in accountancy and racing experience have given him a unique outlook. "I have a strange mix of skills," he says. "Accountancy taught me to be prudent and racing is all about taking things to the limit. I have also benefited from a huge slice of luck. The more I practise, the luckier I get."

Wallpaper trader on a roll with design on glory

**Original interview
3 May 1998**

Frank Cohen's future in the DIY trade was cut and dried after meeting a market trader in a chip shop.

Frank Cohen was determined to leave school and start earning money as soon as he could. Forty years on he probably has more than he needs as owner of Glyn Webb, a chain of 18 home-improvement stores in the north of England.

Cohen, who gained his experience of retailing as a teenager on a market stall, has been a serial entrepreneur but Glyn Webb is his biggest venture to date. Founded in 1972, it is one of Britain's fastest-growing private firms and featured in The 1997 Sunday Times/ Virgin Atlantic Fast Track 100 survey.

Cohen's motive for taking a Saturday job selling tinned food from a stall in St John's market, Liverpool, was to earn money to buy cigarette cards. But he also liked the buzz of trading and he did not want to follow his father, a waterproofs machinist, to work in a raincoat factory.

He left school at 15, determined to work for himself, but knew he needed to learn the tricks of the trade before going it alone. His first break came one Saturday night when he met a market trader called David Riser in a fish 'n' chip shop. Riser had just left the army and was auctioning wallpaper from the back of a van. "Riser was looking for a floor-man, someone who hands out the wallpaper and takes the money. He paid me £2 a week, which was never going to make me rich but was key to teaching me the wallpaper game, and sparking my interest in selling. Riser gave me a focus and the ambition to start up my own stall, and was crucial to my business in years to come."

After two years Cohen had saved £150, enough to buy an old red ambulance and some stock — 'seconds' wallpaper with slight imperfections. He then left Riser and drove around markets hawking wallpaper from the back of his ambulance. He says: "I was soon working 14 markets a week, and was able to afford another van and a salesman to sell from it. The ambulance was invaluable — I made it round the markets in record time as traffic moved out of my way wherever I went. I became a major buyer of seconds wallpaper."
He was making a good income but the business moved up a gear when Cohen met Lionel Berens, owner of a Bolton

household ornaments shop, at an auction. Berens had always wanted to go into wallpaper and Cohen started to supply him. After a few months they hit upon an innovative money-making scheme, which Cohen says was the turning point in his career.

"We had this idea to start DIY exhibitions in town halls and old cinemas around the country where we would discount wallpaper, and gather together a few other salesmen to turn it into a mini-Ideal Home Exhibition," he says. "We would advertise in the local papers and built up quite a following. We became partners and did this for three years, taking a great deal of money — £20,000 a week — not a bad amount in 1964."

Simultaneously, the pair opened one of the first discount wallpaper shops in the country, in Manchester, and soon built it up into a chain of 20, selling paints and other DIY goods.

Unfortunately the two men fell out over strategy in 1972. B&Q and Texas were opening up large warehouse-style DIY stores on 40,000 sq ft sites and Cohen wanted to emulate them to remain competitive, but Berens refused, so the pair decided to split the business and go their separate ways.

But then Cohen had a stroke of luck. He bumped into Riser, who said he was struggling with a wallpaper-manufacturing business he had started and agreed to give Cohen half the company if he could turn it around. Within a year it was making a healthy profit. "The factory had 10,000 sq ft of spare storage space on the second floor. I had an idea that we should open a

factory shop selling all our seconds direct to the public. It was the warehouse store I had always wanted."

He called it the Glyn Webb Home Improvement Store and within a few months he had opened a second outlet in an old mill. He then wound down the manufacturing and retailing became the core business. The company grew steadily and by 1992 it had profits of £540,000 on sales of £5.3m, with a staff of 65. In 1998 it had 19 stores, some at 50,000 sq ft, with three more planned. They are mainly in the north and Midlands but the company, which now employs 550

> ## 'Riser gave me a focus and the ambition to start up my own stall.'

people, is looking to expand nationally over the next few years.

In 1997 Cohen declared a profit of £426,000 on sales of £25m. Cohen bought out Riser earlier in 1998 to own 90% of the business, with staff owning the rest.

Cohen says his success has come from trusting his gut feelings. "I'm a late starter," he says. "I always knew what I wanted to do, but I had to start with the small shops to get to the big ones. You've got to have confidence in what you're doing, otherwise you've had it. If someone kicks you in the teeth don't cry in the corner. Business is about having fun. You will only succeed if you have a feeling for it."

'I'm a late starter. I always knew what I wanted to do, but I had to start with the small shops to get to the big ones.'

Name: **Frank Cohen**

Date of Birth
15 October 1943

Nationality
British

Present Company
Glyn Webb Home Improvement Stores

Age when first in business
17

Education
Chorlton Grammar School, Chorlton, Manchester

Early entrepreneurial ventures
Market trader; Manchester and London Coin Auction Company; Regency Ltd trading in antique reproduction furniture; Home Improvement Company retailing/manufacturing wallpaper; Tiara Tap Tops manufacturing injection moulded tap tops

School holiday job
Worked on market stalls selling a variety of products

Qualifications
—

First job
Selling vacuum cleaners door-to-door for Norvac Electric's

Sales/Profit before tax 1997
Turnover of £25m produced £2m profit before tax and director's emoluments

Weeks holiday per year
As often as business permits

Hobbies/Sports/Interests
Collecting modern British paintings and sculpture and Contemporary Art, fine wines, opera and classical music

Idiosyncrasies, eg, car owned
—

Model agency clicked after photo opportunity

**Original interview
1 March 1998**

Falling out with her photographer boss and a chance call to a former work contact led April Ducksbury to co-found Models 1.

For some entrepreneurs a chance event is all it takes to transform the germ of an idea into a business opportunity. This was the case for April Ducksbury, who resigned from her job with a photographer without any idea of what to do next except for the determination somehow to start her own business.

It was pure coincidence that at the very same time a business contact, Jose Fonseca, left English Boy, a model agency where she worked as a booker. Fonseca also had plans to start her own business, but initially the two were not aware of each other's predicament. Yet despite these unpromising circumstances, after a few weeks they united to start Models 1, now one of the top international model agencies, with Yasmin Le Bon, Patsy Kensit and Jerry Hall on its books.

Early on, Ducksbury had drifted into various jobs, as a secretary, an au pair and a British embassy worker. Then, at an art exhibition by her sister, she learnt of an opportunity to work for David Anthony, an up-and-coming young photographer. "Anthony needed someone to look after the studio, and be his secretary," says Ducksbury. "I had never worked in London before, I was broke, and it seemed a good way to see if I liked London and the industry. It was fascinating to see how the fashion business worked.

"After a few months I was speaking to the model agencies regularly and I'd built up a good rapport with Jose at English Boy. She would call up and try to interest me in booking her models — she had just discovered David's talents and was hounding us."

However, the two did not meet, and in 1968 Ducksbury left Anthony after a disagreement. She wanted to set up her own business, but had no idea how to do it or even what it would be.

"I spent three weeks trying to make up my mind what on earth I was going to do," she says. "Then this amazing coincidence occurred. A friend of mine called me from Paris asking if I could recommend a good model agency for him, and, not knowing that Jose had left English Boy, I recommended her. I had no way of contacting her other than through her work number, but as luck would have it, she

Date of Birth
12 April 1932

Nationality
British

Present Company
Models One Ltd

Age when first in business
18

Education
**Private Schools; Finishing School;
Secretarial College**

Early entrepreneurial ventures
—

School holiday job
Petrol station attendant

Qualifications
**2 years working in a film agency;
18 months working for a top
fashion photographer**

First job
Documentary film company

Sales/Profit before tax 1997
Sales: £7.5m Profit £2.2m

Weeks holiday per year
Four weeks

Hobbies/Sports/Interests
Politics

Idiosyncrasies, eg, car owned
**Married at 59 after a
30-year involvement**

'You have to be
patient. I didn't
think about making
money, it came
with the success
of the business.'

had returned to work for one day to tidy up some invoices."

It also transpired that Fonseca had been trying to contact her, but without success. Three of Fonseca's girlfriends — top models Marisa Berenson, Ingrid Boulting and Susan Murray — were trying to encourage her to start her own agency. They were willing to come with her, but Fonseca was concerned she did not have the organisational and financial skills. "I convinced her that she should go for it, and that with my background and her talents we would make a good team," says Ducksbury. "If she had not gone into the office to sort out those invoices, Models 1 would never have happened. We met the next day, and when she told me about the three models joining us — they really were superstars — I knew it would work. We opened up shop the following Monday in her flat."

Models 1 was formed in 1968 and Ducksbury worked out what it would take to keep going for three months, and borrowed $1,000 from her boyfriend, Charles Fawcett, an actor. The overheads were low, but they soon moved to an attic office after a business rival told the council they were using a home for their business. They broke even within four months, and were able to pay back the loan.

After a year they took on a book-keeper and moved to new premises in the Fulham Road. They soon added four bookers and a new faces scout to the team. In 1984 Models 1 for men was opened. In 1985 the business made a profit of £63,000 on sales of £487,000. The agency now employs 30 staff and has 90 women and 70 men on its books. In 1997 it made commissions of £2.2m on sales of £7.5m.

Ducksbury grew up in Huddersfield, West Yorkshire, the daughter of a hotelier. She was educated at St Anthony's, Wallingford, Berkshire. Her mother did not work and thought it was not something girls should have to do. But that made Ducksbury more determined to get a job. She had no qualifications but went to secretarial college after her father threatened to cut off her allowance. She secured her first job as an assistant for a documentary film-production company.

> **'I convinced her that she should go for it, and that with my background and her talents we would make a good team.'**

She says success is down to differentiating the product: "Jose had new ideas. She wanted to keep the agency small and take only prestigious models. Our big asset has been Jose's brilliant eye, and I deal with the rest. Initiative and hard work are important and at the end of the day it helps to get a real kick out of the work. You have to be patient. I didn't think about making money, it came with the success of the business. It's just interesting to see the girls' careers take off, and the agency with them."

'Reassuringly expensive' service put IT ace on map

Original interview
5 July 1998

Advice that low fees would not inspire confidence among potential clients put IDG's Pat McGovern on the road to riches.

Most people try to get into business by undercutting the competition — but not Pat McGovern, the journalist-turned-publisher who owns *PC World* magazine, America's top personal-computer title.

His original research business was started in 1964 after he took advice from a potential customer and decided to raise his price 60% to make his service seem 'reassuringly expensive'. At the time McGovern was a computer-magazine editor but was hungry for his own company. He put together a business plan but found his prices were too low to be taken seriously by potential clients.

McGovern, who now heads International Data Group (IDG), set out on the entrepreneurial trail after interviewing Louis Rader, chief executive of Univac, then the top computer maker after IBM. "Rader needed information on the computer market. He said he had no reliable means of finding out which companies had what equipment or what their future technological needs and objectives might be.

"His only source of knowledge was from his salesforce. Most scarce was information from successful salesmen, who were too busy to do the paperwork and keep him in the picture, whereas there was bountiful information from staff who could not sell and had plenty of time to complete the paperwork. This understandably did not contain much useful material."

Thus McGovern offered to do a computer market analysis based on polling companies about what computers they had and how they were using them. He proposed a fee of $12,500 by using low-cost Massachusetts Institute of Technology (MIT) student labour. "Rader was not impressed and insisted I charge $20,000 for the study so that he would have an easier task convincing his team the information was properly researched and trustworthy," he says. "I thought 'great — charge more and get more clients, this has got to be a winner'." McGovern's own boss rejected this business opportunity so he launched what became IDG, raising $5,000 of capital by selling his car.

Rader's advice about doing quality work and charging a premium for it proved critical. Today McGovern is one of America's richest people, presiding over a business empire that spans publications, books, the Internet, research and conferences. Its 285 magazines include *Playstation* and *Windows 95*, and they sell in 75 countries. In 1997 IDG made operating profits of $240m (£150m) on sales of $2.1 billion, and in June 1998 it floated 25% of its books division.

McGovern grew up in Philadelphia and won an MIT scholarship to study biophysics. He took a holiday job writing for a magazine called *Computers in Automation* and became editor on graduation. His boss, Ed Berkeley, left him to run the magazine and this gave McGovern the chance to learn about the business of publishing. After four years interviewing computer bosses he decided he also wanted to be an entrepreneur.

Working in his spare time, McGovern sent research proposals to 10 computer suppliers, most of which he knew through his job. Within a day, eight returned cheques for $10,000 as deposits on their subscriptions, yet he did not even have a bank account into which to put them.

McGovern's MIT student workers sent out questionnaires and collated results, initially to produce data twice a year. Within three years sales had grown to $1m and he quit his job to build his business full time, turning his output into a weekly publication. In 1967 he started publishing a weekly newspaper, *Computer World*, believing there was room for an independent title.

The magazines of the day, he says, were "little more than propaganda sheets". Starting with $50,000 of savings, he took an aggressive stance, challenging the industry. Rivals laughed at him and warned he would need at least $1m to make the venture work but they were wrong. "It took just a few months before readers found it was the first time they were getting the truth and advertisers reluctantly booked space with us because of this."

Within two years IDG had 60 staff, profits of $400,000 and sales of $5m, and McGovern was confident enough to expand in research and publishing, rolling out fresh titles in Europe and Asia. Today IDG employs 12,000 staff,

> **'I thought "great — charge more and get more clients, this has got to be a winner".'**

yet maintains a flat organisational structure with each country's head reporting to IDG's executive committee headed by McGovern. In the future it may be split into separate businesses that will be progressively floated over the next 10 years.

McGovern sees himself as "cheerleader for the company". He says: "I had a belief early on that computers could really change people's lives. The key has been not to do too much long-term planning and burden myself with perceived problems that almost never happen. That stifles entrepreneurialism and is an unnecessary diversion."

Date of Birth
11 August 1937

Nationality
American

Present Company
International Data Group

Age when first in business
27

Education
BS degree in Biophysics from Massachusetts Institute of Technology

Early entrepreneurial ventures
Delivered newspapers; painted homes during high school and ran a business building science lab projects for upperclassmen

School holiday job
Associate Editor of computer magazine

Qualifications
—

First job
Associate Editor of the first computer magazine Computers in Automation

Sales/Profit before tax 1997
Sales: $2.1 billion Profit: $240m

Weeks holiday per year
Three weeks

Hobbies/Sports/Interests
Mountain biking, tennis, mountain climbing, adventure travel

Idiosyncrasies, eg, car owned
Drives 12-year-old Mercedes; did a skydive from an airplane to illustrate "Let's try it" principle; travelled to the South Pole to launch Computerworld Antarctica, **to become the first publishing company to launch magazines on all seven continents**

'I had a belief early on that computers could really change people's lives.'

Sexy salesman got Janet Reger going

Original interview
31 May 1998

Her sexy underwear was taken by Harrods and Fenwicks after buyers mistook her husband for a salesman they fancied.

A case of mistaken identity helped Janet Reger launch her racy underwear business. She spent years as a freelance lingerie designer anonymously creating bras and panty girdles for high-street chains while dreaming of creating her own label.

But she only managed to secure her first order because underwear buyers at Harrods and Fenwicks mistook her Reger name for a more established label. The business, which she called Janet Reger, grew in the 1970s as women (or their men) demanded sexy underwear not available elsewhere. She eventually created an international brand worn around the world.

Reger opened four stores — two in London, one in Bond Street, the other in Beauchamp Place, Knightsbridge — and at the peak in 1981 she made £600,000 on sales of £2m. In 1983, Reger over-expanded at a time of weak consumer demand and her company was forced into liquidation.

But she did not give up: she borrowed £25,000 from her family to rescue parts of it and today she operates out of one shop and a factory.

She plans to avoid over-expansion this time around but she is building her brand again — in 1993 she took her range to America and it is now stocked in Saks Fifth Avenue and Neiman-Marcus. She employs 50 staff and made £64,704 profit on sales of £967,855 in 1997.

Reger graduated from Leicester College of Art, now part of De Montfort University, as a talented designer but her career only took off after she met Peter Reger, a German, on a kibbutz. He added business skills to her design talent and later became her husband.

"Peter was studying chemistry in Munich and I went there to live with him. I started designing swimwear and underwear for companies but became pregnant and had to carry on at home doing freelance work. I created some garments for shops but always felt a little frightened at the business side. I gave in easily in negotiations and then Peter would shout at me. But once I'd started working for myself I could never contemplate working for anyone

Date of Birth
30 September 1935

Nationality
British

Present Company
Janet Reger

Age when first in business
23/24

Education
**Kendrick Grammar School;
Leicester College of Art**

Early entrepreneurial ventures
—

School holiday job
Littlewoods, Lyons Café

Qualifications
—

First job
**Swimwear and lingerie
company at St Margaret's Street**

Sales/Profit before tax 1997
Sales: £967,855 Profit: £64,704

Weeks holiday per year
—

Hobbies/Sports/Interests
Reading, travelling, swimming

Idiosyncrasies, eg, car owned
BMW

**'It's a bit like starting
out with a new lover
— he needs to be
looked after and
treated well.
Otherwise you'll
lose him.'**

else again. Suddenly that all seemed too constrictive."

Peter Reger would spend his lunchtimes typing letters and negotiating rates for his wife's work and as a result of his work the sales began to grow. In 1966 the Regers moved to England with a plan that Janet would continue freelancing. But her husband thought they could be more ambitious.

"There was not enough work for Peter to give up his job, and too much work for him to help me in his spare time, so we decided to manufacture our own garments with our own label, Janet Reger."

Peter Reger stuffed a suit case with samples and began visiting shops. At first he found it hard to get appointments at department stores. But when he approached Harrods and Fenwicks the buyers fell over themselves to meet him. Reger says: "Store buyers were reluctant to see new collections but the buyers mistook my husband on the telephone for a very good-looking importer with a similar name, Rabi, whom they all had the hots for. All it took was a foot in the door and as soon as they saw my collection they said 'At last, something that's pretty' and placed orders. We never looked back."

Reger designed collections, organised manufacturing and was soon employing five people in a room above a Paddington garage and contracting out to 20 seamstresses working from home. In its first year the business broke even on sales of £40,000. It then doubled in size for the next five years and in 1974 the Knightsbridge shop opened. Reger started a factory in Derby, whose costs she funded out of cashflow over two years, and began showing her collection in Paris and New York.

By 1977 she had four stores and was employing 120 people, but within a few years she was in deep trouble. "I learnt the most about my business when we liquidated it," she says. "With hindsight I could see how the sharks, the lawyers and accountants were trying to refinance it; it was total misery."

She bought the factory and some stock and kept the Knightsbridge shop and set about restoring her business reputa-

> **'But once I'd started working for myself I could never contemplate working for anyone else again.'**

tion. She has succeeded and the company has recently been strengthened by the arrival of her daughter, Aliza, who took over the day-to-day running of the business last year.

Reger says that being positive, patient and hardworking has yielded results. "When starting a business you need to be self-sacrificing," she says. "It's a bit like starting out with a new lover — he needs to be looked after and treated well. Otherwise you'll lose him."

Boy racer discovers the winning formula

**Original interview
17 May 1998**

As a nine-year-old dirt-track racer, Adrian Reynard not only showed promise on the circuit, he also discovered a talent for making money.

It was a childhood passion for anything with a motor, and an uncanny knack for making money, that have been instrumental in making Adrian Reynard's fortune. But even Reynard could not do it by himself.

His first break came after a chance meeting with fellow motor-racing enthusiast, Bill Stone, when he was setting up a motor-racing club at his college. Stone later invested £30 in their joint company. Reynard put in a lathe and some welding gear. The pair went on to make racing cars, and when Stone emigrated to New Zealand in 1977, Reynard took over what has become Reynard Motorsport, a motor-racing business.

It now consists of 12 engineering, electronics, and manufacturing divisions and its profile will be significantly boosted in 1999 when it teams up with British American Racing, the new Formula One team that bought Tyrrell. Reynard will become technical director and assume control of design,

development and manufacturing. The group now employs 230 people and made £8.5m in 1998 on sales of £38m.

The nine-year-old boy who was given a moped by his great uncle and became hooked on dirt-track racing has come a long way. Reynard sold the bike after learning an early marketing lesson: he put a spoonful of castor oil in the petrol tank to give it a racing smell.

He went on to make a small fortune while he was still a teenager by buying and selling bikes. Reynard had a tough time at school, putting in the minimum amount of effort and being less than academic. But he placated his teachers by working on their cars. "I had bought and sold about 100 bikes by the time I was 17 and moved on to cars. I rebuilt the maths teacher's car. I started a small enterprise, mobile welding, charging £1 an hour."

The business was not without its ups and downs. Once, when he was welding a car, his blowtorch set fire to its carpets and the interior went up in smoke. Needless to say he did not get paid.

In 1969 Reynard started an apprenticeship with British Leyland, where he attended an HND course at Oxford Polytechnic. While he was there he broke five world land speed records on a motorbike. At college he realised that students could get a £100 grant for starting student societies, so he set up an automobile club.

On a club outing to March Engineering, which ran a Formula One team, he met Stone, the March production manager. The rapport was immediate. Stone was interested in Reynard's racing skills and followed his career. "We would talk about making money and I told him about my dreams and aspirations," says Reynard. "I had always wanted to create a proper business around the various schemes I had going. I have never been the sort of person that works well for other people; I am not a con-formist. Bill said we should go into business together, with me designing, and him doing the manufacturing."

They called the firm Sabre Automotive. Reynard stayed at Leyland, designing Sabre's car parts in his spare time because the business could not support two salaries. Stone left March and started making the parts. Sabre soon won contracts to sup-ply March and found premises in a for-mer undertaker's yard. Reynard started to design racing cars as well, which Stone made in kit form because the pair did not have the space to assemble them in the yard.

By 1977 the business was making £25,000 on a turnover of £250,000 and employing 10 people. Reynard bought Stone out and renamed the business.

He started a Formula 2000 racing team and was soon making most of the cars used by his competitors. He borrowed £90,000 from NatWest to build a new factory, and in 1985 moved Reynard into Formula 3. The business turned over £1.2m. This soared to £3m in 1988 when economies of scale kicked in and his margins improved to 20%.

Late in 1993, Reynard moved into Indycar racing (now the ChampCar series) where he supplies three-quarters of the field. He has since established other businesses including Reynard Aviation, Reynard Special Vehicle Projects, and Reynard Composites.

> **'We would talk about making money and I told him my dreams and aspirations.'**

He says a zest for life and doing as much as possible in the areas he feels passionate about are key to success. "Persistence and determination are important," he says. "None of my staff are ever satisfied with the job we do. We try to be aware of all imperfections and this tends to bond us together as an effective team. I like to surround myself with a group of specialists rather than all-rounders."

Name: **Adrian Reynard**

Date of Birth
23 March 1951

Nationality
British

Present Company
Reynard Motorsport Ltd

Age when first in business
Buying and selling motorcycles, aged 13; Sabre Automotive Ltd, aged 20

Education
**Alleynes Grammar School, 1962–68;
Oxford Polytechnic, 1969–73;
Cranfield Institute Technology, 1974–75**

Early entrepreneurial ventures
Car maintenance and chassis welding

School holiday job
Work in local motorcycle shop (George Brown, Stevenage)

Qualifications
D Eng, FI Mech E, FRSA, CRAeS, C Eng

First job
British Leyland research and development engineer

Sales/Profit before tax 1997
**(1998) Sales: £38m
(1998) Profit: £8.5m**

Weeks holiday per year
Five to six weeks

Hobbies/Sports/Interests
Flying, water-skiing, family and children, boating, karting for kids, clay pigeon shooting, motorcycling, scuba diving

Idiosyncrasies, eg, car owned
Mainly pickup trucks, Dodge Ram 1500. Always fly economy. Casual clothes, long hair

A Gap In The Market

Jonathan Elvidge
gadgets

David Potter
palmtop computers

Kate Bleasdale
healthcare management

Theo Fennell
jewellery

Dean Butler
eye care

Henry Lewis
mail order computer retailing

Santa inspires Gadget Shop founder

**Original interview
14 September 1997**

Jonathan Elvidge could not find a store that sold innovative presents, so in 1991 he decided to open his own. Today he runs a chain of 25.

Jonathan Elvidge wanted to run his own company as a boy and began his business career as a child entrepreneur. At 14 he had a business selling brushes on council estates, and at 17 he appeared on television news after winning an award as young engineer of the year for co-designing kitchen scales for the blind.

"I knew we had a better chance if we created something worthy," he says. "It's all about identifying whom you target."

He fell on an idea he could make into a proper business some years later. He had left his Christmas shopping too late and was trying to find a retailer that stocked a large range of innovative presents. He found none and realised there was a gap.

After two years of research, he decided to start such a business himself and opened The Gadget Shop at the new Princes Quay shopping centre in Hull in 1991.

Before the year was out he had opened two more shops and now has 25. His 1998 accounts will show profits of £3m, up from £1m in 1997, on sales of £16m, up from £12.2m in 1997 — they had previously doubled in each of the past three years.

His aspiration to be an entrepreneur came after a number of diversions and a series of make-or-break situations. He failed to complete his A-levels and followed his brother into the Hull Telephone Department, now Kingston Communications, as an apprentice telephone engineer while he decided what to do.

"I used the time to get my bearings," he says. "At first they had me digging holes, but I had to be rescued when the pneumatic drill took off down the road with me.

"Then I was up poles where I learnt a lesson that has always stuck with me — if you tread in muck on the way up, you get it on your hands on the way down. Holes and poles taught me to understand people from the ground up."

Elvidge worked his way around the company and after a spell in technical support he moved to sales. "I found I

Date of Birth
2 November 1963

Nationality
British

Present Company
The Gadget Shop Ltd

Age when first in business
27 (full time)

Education
**'O' levels and HND in telecomms
engineering.**

Early entrepreneurial ventures
**Commercial photography on
part-time basis**

School holiday job
Selling Betterware door-to-door

Qualifications
**Telecommunications HND;
Winner of Young Engineer for
Britain award**

First job
Apprentice telephone engineer

Sales/Profit before tax 1997
Sales: £12.2m Profit: £1m

Weeks holiday per year
Two weeks

Hobbies/Sports/Interests
Flying

Idiosyncrasies, eg, car owned
**Always carries a selection of
gadgets and only ever wears black;
drives favourite car, Porsche 911**

**'You have to be
prepared to lose
everything and
remember that the
biggest risk is
not taking any risk.'**

was accompanying salesmen to new-business meetings and would explain products' capabilities, only for the salesmen to pocket the commission after I had effectively won the sale. Selling was not new to me. The brush business had sharpened my communication skills and confidence."

He rose to be a star salesman but found inspiration from reading books about how entrepreneurs started out in business. His plans for the gift shop were accelerated when he fell out with a Kingston sales manager, who moved him sideways.

He drew up a business plan for his new venture and spent his holidays travelling to gift conventions. "People used to think, 'Here comes that nutter again; it's the imaginary shop man'," he says. "I got friends at work to carry out market research and used the office laser printer to make letter-headings with my new logo."

Elvidge's perseverance paid off. He remortgaged his new home — he had sold the previous one at the top of the 1980s housing boom — and raised enough money to fund his first shop.

It was then that a feature in the local press alerted his employers Kingston Communications to what Elvidge was up to and he was told to choose between the jobs. He chose to leave the company but, when his initial launch was delayed, he hit a crisis.

"I missed out on the Christmas sales, which dented my cashflow projections. I needed to raise a further £20,000 or

face going under before I had even opened my doors."

But Elvidge responded by visiting his library and finding a book about how Sock Shop's Sophie Mirman raised cash through the small firms loan-guarantee scheme, under which the government guarantees 70% of a loan.

Elvidge then convinced NatWest to help him and launched his shop. "From the day it opened, The Gadget Shop was a success," he says. "After five months it made a small profit on £200,000 of sales, but I did not want to be just a shopkeeper and I did want to open another branch."

> **'I knew we had a better chance if we created something worthy. It's all about identifying whom you target.'**

He soon found a partner, Andrew Hobbs, who had seen a plan for the first store because he acted on behalf of the letting agents of the shopping centre. He invested capital to help the business expand, and by 1993 the company was making healthy profits.

Elvidge says being ordinary and in tune with his customers is the key to his success. "There is no such thing as a half-hearted entrepreneur," he says. "You have to be prepared to lose everything and remember that the biggest risk is not taking any risk."

Psion's Potter took off with flight simulator

Original interview
1 June 1997

Success with a game for home computers gave David Potter the resources to set up his palmtop computer company.

David Potter's business took off when he invested £100,000 made from playing the stock market in developing an early home computer flight-simulator game.

The game earned him a fortune and was the break that Potter needed to get his business off the ground. Today he is chairman of Psion, the palmtop computer maker.

In 17 years, Psion, which stood originally for Potter Scientific Instruments Or Nothing, has grown into a £350m company, expanding from software into palmtop personal organisers — the Psion is the Filofax of the 1990s, and Potter's personal fortune now stands at £90m.

The company employs 1,000 people, has offices in Boston, Amsterdam and Frankfurt, and distributes to 45 countries. While Potter's first break came from the flight simulator, he acquired his business skills in less high-tech jobs — as a lorry driver and ice-cream vendor.

Born in the South African port of East London and brought up in Cape Town, he moved to England after winning a natural-sciences scholarship to Trinity College, Cambridge.

"I was always involved in projects where I sold things," says Potter. "The scholarship did not cover living expenses, and I had to earn a living during the holidays.

"There was a huge diversity of wealth at Cambridge but I was this strange colonial character they could not pigeonhole. I think I learnt about as much through my jobs as I did through my studies. I drove lorries in the days when you did not need a heavy goods licence. I travelled all over Britain delivering to retailers, and would drive intensively for the first part of the week to ensure I had a couple of days off in London at the end. I picked up a great deal about a cross-section of Britain and it paid very well."

One summer Potter sold encyclopedias to American soldiers in Germany. It helped him with his sales skills but made him feel guilty. "Americans take their children's education very seriously and many found it difficult to say no even when it was clear they could not afford the $500. I learnt about character and human nature."

When he decided to try to make it big as an ice-cream vendor, he nearly came a cropper. Fellow students sold ice cream in the suburban back streets but Potter thought he would go for the big bucks in Hyde Park, unaware that prime spots are jealously guarded by career ice-cream men.

"I muscled in through complete ignorance and did rather well," he says. "But some regulars took a different view and I was marched off and taught a lesson. I got off lightly as I heard stories of less fortunate entrepreneurs being kidnapped. I had a very independent childhood where I almost brought myself up. It gave me a large amount of self-confidence to be able to deal with things."

Potter's father died when he was a baby: "Half of successful chief executives lost their fathers at an early age," he says. He was brought up by his mother, a nurse, and his grandmother. He was a bright child and studied at Bishops School in Cape Town, and Prince Edward School in Zimbabwe where he took his A-levels.

After Cambridge he did a doctorate at Imperial College, London in theoretical physics, and he began to use computers. He also studied in Los Angeles around the time Silicon Valley was being established.

He says: "Colleagues had a computer in their garage when only the likes of British Gas and the Ministry of Defence had them in Britain. The

microchip came along and I could see a world where computers would be the future. My ambition was to build a substantial enterprise."

Potter made a small fortune by gambling £3,000 of his savings on the stock market, and found his business and technical skills came together in Psion. He bought a small office in Maida Vale, north London, and in 1979 started to publish computer software — the flight simulator was his first big success.

The company mushroomed, from sales of £1.6m in its second year to £30m after nine years and £140m in 1997. In

> **'Half of successful chief executives lost their fathers at an early age.'**

August of that year it brought out its latest palmtop organiser: the five series.

He says there is no single key to business success. "You need to be adventurous in a business sense and conservative in a financial way. It is important to take a long-term view with a business plan but while the plan needs to be strong it also needs to be flexible," he says. "For us the key is to follow what the customer wants. Nothing replaces hard work and the fusion of identifying a market opportunity with technology evolution."

Date of Birth
4 July 1943

Nationality
South African

Present Company
Psion Plc

Age when first in business
Early twenties

Education
Natural Sciences at Trinity College, Cambridge; Mathematical Physics at Imperial College, University of London

Early entrepreneurial ventures
Lorry driver, ice-cream seller, encyclopaedia seller

School holiday job
—

Qualifications
PhD, MS Bc

First job
Academic at University of London

Sales/Profit before tax 1997
Sales: £140m Profit: £11m

Weeks holiday per year
Varies — approximately six weeks

Hobbies/Sports/Interests
Tennis, gardening, and playing the flute

Idiosyncrasies, eg, car owned
BMW 735i

'Nothing replaces hard work and the fusion of identifying a market opportunity with technology evolution.'

Nurse found cure for staff shortages

Original interview
24 May 1998

Kate Bleasdale's plan for staffing hospitals efficiently was ignored by the NHS, so she set it up as a business.

Turning what seems a winning new idea into a business is the first challenge faced by would-be enterpreneurs. Such was the experience of Kate Bleasdale, the former nurse who now heads Sinclair Montrose Healthcare, the £37m quoted group that runs an employment agency and private doctor's surgeries.

Bleasdale's idea was to create a computer program to satisfy hospital wards' staffing needs by providing them with good nurses, which she intended to recruit through her own employment agency.

But having conceived the idea in 1986 with her then colleague, now husband, John Cariss, she needed a sale within the National Health Service to give the embryonic business credibility.

She trawled her nursing contacts, even before the computer program was complete, and eventually persuaded the nursing director at St Heliers Hospital in Carlshalton to install a system. Bleasdale had to offer a discount price of £20,000 but she negotiated the right to use St Heliers as a show site. The system was an instant success. St Heliers and soon other hospitals were making cost savings and after a year of start-up losses Bleasdale, who remortgaged her house to pay for hardware, was in profit.

Bleasdale thought of her idea after becoming frustrated with the constraints of her job as a nursing manager at the Putney Hospital in London. At the time she was only 25 but had to organise a staff of 120. She found she spent all her time sorting out staffing rotas and finding replacement nurses. She was also acutely aware that she would have to wait 10 years for promotion within the NHS.

She says: "I have always been a bit of a maverick. I don't think I have ever been very comfortable working within an organisation. I didn't think I was cut out to bide my time and work my way up the ladder, so I began to look for an opportunity to be my own boss."

Her idea was prompted by an experience one Saturday when she turned up for work at 7am and found there were not enough nurses. She did a trawl of agencies, ringing about 10, knowing

Date of Birth
10 January 1961

Nationality
British

Present Company
Sinclair Montrose Healthcare Plc

Age when first in business
26

Education
**Convent Grammar School;
University of London**

Early entrepreneurial ventures
**Set up nurse bank system Match
Healthcare Services**

School holiday job
Shoe salesgirl

Qualifications
**BSc (Hons) in nursing, MSc in
nursing research**

First job
Staff nurse

Sales/Profit before tax 1997
Sales: £19,089,000 Profit: £647,000

Weeks holiday per year
Four weeks

Hobbies/Sports/Interests
**Looking after four sons, skiing,
tennis**

Idiosyncrasies, eg, car owned
**Own Jaguar XK8 sports car, and
am known for sticking to my guns**

**'There seemed to be

a real need,

and I knew it was

not a problem

peculiar to us.'**

she would get less experienced nurses from smaller more obscure agencies.

She found cover but then saw an agency nurse walk past an old man with Alzheimer's disease, ignoring his request for help. The nurse said she did not help the man because he was not assigned to her.

"I ended up working two and a half shifts as well as being on call for two other hospitals. I thought, there must be a better way. I started to build up a register of part-time and seasonal nurses with details of ability and availability. I knew they were high quality because I had hand-picked them. And I thought a better way to manage them would be through a computerised system. There seemed to be a real need, and I knew it was not a problem peculiar to us. If staffing was a full-time job for me, it would be for other nursing managers up and down the country."

Bleasdale created a business plan after talking to computer companies about programs to match staff with the wards' needs, and presented a paper to the hospital board. But the board did nothing, so Bleasdale quit and did it herself.

She teamed up with Cariss, then a hospital manager. The two borrowed £5,000 each from their parents, got a £10,000 bank loan and began trading as a staff agency while the program was written.

By 1990 the company had sales of £330,000. It had 30,000 nurses on its books and had seven contracts for the computer system. Five years later sales were at £2.2m and Bleasdale was sufficiently ambitious to merge with an agency for placing general practitioners run by Mike Sinclair.

In 1994 Bleasdale diversified into medicentres, an idea she spotted on holiday in America. Doctors' surgeries are sited in places such as stations and shopping centres, enabling patients to walk in without appointments. So far there are eleven. The company floated on the Alternative Investment Market in 1996 and has since made four takeovers.

> **'I didn't think I was cut out to work my way up the ladder, so I began to look for an opportunity to be my own boss.'**

In May 1998, the company, which has 700 staff and made a pre-tax profit of £647,000 in 1997, launched a medical insurance scheme offering private consultations with doctors.

Bleasdale says the keys to success are drive, determination and stamina, and getting things right more often than wrong.

Third time lucky for jeweller who struck gold

**Original interview
15 March 1998**

A gold champagne flute inscribed 'Good Morning Diana' showed Theo Fennell there was a market for trinkets that are fun as well as beautiful.

Sometimes it takes more than one attempt to start a successful business. For Theo Fennell, the London jeweller, it took three before he found the right formula to keep the business going and make money.

But his first break came years before, when he was unsure of which career to take up. A chance event sparked his interest in jewellery, and within a few months he had spotted an opportunity that would form the basis for his own business.

It all began after Fennell left Eton to study fine art and painting at Byam Shaw, a college in Kensington, London. He applied for work through a job centre for public schoolboys and was taken on at Edward Barnard, a silversmith founded in the 17th century. Fennell had once had ideas of being a soldier, astronaut or England cricketer. Now he was employed to do much less glamorous work, cataloguing repairs and filing. He had never been greatly interested in working with precious metals, but one day an item was brought in that caught his imagination.

"A lot of dull items came in to be melted, and I spotted this gold champagne flute engraved with 'Good Morning Diana'. It was beautifully made, as well as being witty and louche. It was both intimate, and symbolic, implying that the first thing this Diana would do when she woke up was drink champagne. I was intrigued that someone would go to so much trouble to have such an inconsequential item made."

It give him the idea that there could be a market waiting to be tapped. With imagination, he could add value to ordinary items. After a year Fennell was finding the company claustrophobic. He had suggested a range of what he thought were innovative ideas, only to be rebuffed. "It was a family firm with solid clients and had sold the same products for centuries." Fennell's opportunity to follow his entrepreneurial instincts came when he was approached by James Grimshaw, a trader who regularly brought in pieces for repair.

He needed a large number of goblets made, but Barnard was not interested in the new business and banned

Fennell from doing the work in his spare time. He decided to go freelance. "I told Grimshaw I could do it, and we formed a loose partnership using his office across the road as a base. I did not know what an invoice was or have a clue about business, so I designed and he brought in the clients. Two older guys in a workshop next to me taught me the patience and skill of making jewellery. I made bits and bobs for friends and relatives to begin with."

Grimshaw retired after two years and Fennell took over the lease of the business, employing the two older men and selling jewellery in Portobello Road market. When the lease ran out, he borrowed £2,000 from Coutts and leased a condemned house in Islington, taking on an apprentice and touring friends' houses in the evenings with a briefcase full of his work. He won a contract to churn out limited-edition miniatures sold through the colour supplements, and employed two more workers. But Fennell found the work was not regular enough to sustain the staff and the rent.

"My business inexperience caught up with me," he says. This was compounded by a second problem. "I had a safe in the house protected by Rebel, an albino Alsatian, which looked quite frightening. But one night we had a break-in. The safe was missing and so was Rebel."

Fennell wound up his business. But he had quite a following of clients and in 1980 a group of friends were going to put up £100,000 to open his first shop carrying his name. However, one rela-tive stranger took over the onus of financing it himself but never quite put his money where his mouth was. The business went into liquidation but his suppliers remained faithful and he was able to start up again, third time lucky.

Richard Northcott, a friend, helped Fennell buy the assets of the previous shop but had the sense to put in an accountant as finance director. Fennell concentrated on design. The workshop was doubled in size, and the business benefited from a prime location on Fulham Road. A small catalogue was produced and Fennell, inspired by the champagne flute, designed unusual

> **'I was intrigued that someone would go to so much trouble to have such an item made.'**

gifts such as silver Marmite jar tops and silver tomato ketchup holders.

Another early break was being invited to open a boutique in Harrods. Fennell's profile grew, and he expanded from employing 12 staff in 1985 to 60 in 1997. In 1996 he floated on the Alternative Investment Market and is now looking for opportunities abroad. In 1997, Theo Fennell made profits of £1m on sales of £10m.

He says his later success is due to learning the practicalities of running a business. "Flair and talent can only take you so far," he says. "Self-belief is important — you have to commit yourself utterly, even when everything around you tells you otherwise."

Date of Birth
8 August 1951

Nationality
British

Present Company
Theo Fennell Plc

Age when first in business
25

Education
Eton; Byam Shaw

Early entrepreneurial ventures
All silver and jewellery based

School holiday job
**None at school, but many and
various from art school**

Qualifications
Few

First job
Edward Barnard & Sons

Sales/Profit before tax 1997
Sales: £10m Profit: £1m

Weeks holiday per year
Never more than a week at a time

Hobbies/Sports/Interests
**Golf, cricket, reading, drawing,
popular music (1880-1970)**

Idiosyncrasies, eg, car owned
Do not drive

'Self-belief is important — you have to commit yourself utterly, even when everything around you tells you otherwise.'

Vision Express chief has eye for an opportunity

**Original interview
4 May 1997**

When Dean Butler's wife was turned away by an optician he sought revenge and started what became Vision Express.

Vision is not something Dean Butler lacks. The former chairman of Vision Express, the high-street optician, is an enthusiast who loves talking about his vintage racing cars. But he is also a moneymaker.

He may be short-sighted physically but he has been singularly focused on achieving success. He has pioneered the one-hour spectacle superstore and has built ventures in America, Australia and Europe. Today Vision Express has more than 200 stores and the pre-tax profits showed a rise from £8.1m to £19.5m in 1995 on sales up from £80.6m to £99.3m. He owned 30% of the company, which paid a £4m dividend in that year. But, in 1998 Butler sold Vision Express and now heads Winning Vision Services.

Butler became involved in the optician business while at Procter & Gamble in Cincinnati. A combination of spite and good nature sparked his interest. "I had a friend, John Cutrer, who was in field sales with me at Procter & Gamble," he says. "His father-in-law passed away and left him five old-fashioned optical stores in Baton Rouge, Louisiana.

"There were big changes in the industry at the time. The Federal Trade Commission ruled that customers should be given a copy of their prescription so they could get it filled wherever they chose, pretty much breaking up a centuries-old conflict of interest. Opticians were also allowed to advertise."

A rival's advertising campaign hurt Cutrer and he asked Butler to dream up some advertisements for him. "I did him a favour, which, as it turned out, has more than worked to my advantage. We shot the first commercial and it brought in an extra £100,000 worth of revenue. I returned every six months for four years to write the latest commercials." Butler explored the idea of making glasses within one hour and found that it was possible but needed a lab in each store. He and Cutrer visited a rival who had installed equipment but was offering only a two-day service. Cutrer wanted to set up a lab in Baton Rouge if Butler would do the advertising. Thus Eye Masters was born and within days it was America's top-selling optician.

Name: **Dean Butler**

Date of Birth
—

Nationality
American

Present Company
Winning Vision Services Ltd

Age when first in business
First owned business at 37

Education
BS (Chemistry, Physics), MS (Chemistry), MBA (International Marketing)

Early entrepreneurial ventures
Lens Crafters, aged 37

School holiday job
Worked in a steel mill

Qualifications
NOT a qualified optician

First job
Dipping ice-cream cones, aged 15

Sales/Profit before tax 1997
—

Weeks holiday per year
No idea — do not think of anything as a holiday

Hobbies/Sports/Interests
Race historic grand prix cars (1938 Maserati 8CTF, 1931 Maserati 26M, 1931 Type 51 Bugatti, 1934 MG K3)

Idiosyncrasies, eg, car owned
Drive TVR Griffith and 4.5 Cerbera as everyday cars

'Having the idea is easy. Getting the guts to go out and do it is the hard part.'

But the turning point in Butler's career did not come until his wife went for an eye test at a local optician called Manney Commissar with a view to buying glasses at Eye Masters and returned home crying because Commissar refused the test unless she bought from him. "None of the bodies I complained to would act. So I thought, 'I'm going to teach this guy a lesson and open a store like John's'. I left Procter & Gamble in 1982, remortgaged the house, and started Lens Crafters with help from John. My wife was pregnant with our first child and thought I'd gone mad. We opened just down the road from Commissar and were profitable from day one.

"We grew to four stores within three years. The US Shoe Corporation then offered to buy Lens Crafters for $7.5m. We had invested $750,000 and didn't have the money to expand it, and knew they would only set up their own chain, so we sold." Butler negotiated a 2% cut of the profits for five years, and helped the chain grow to 231 stores with $43m of profit on sales of about $400m.

He became a wealthy man but could not set up in competition, so he took the concept to Europe and Australia under the Vision Express name. In 1991 he sold out of Australia for about £5m and decided to focus on Europe.

Born in Philadelphia, the son of an advertising executive, Butler was a gifted child, who never had to work hard to get top exam marks. "I have a qualitative mind," he says. "I can glance at a balance sheet and spot anomalies from the relationship between figures. I have to stop doing it as it unnerves my finance team."

After taking degrees in physics and chemistry, he became a chemist at a local chemical company and then planned to work in Procter & Gamble's research department. But there was a mix-up at his interview and he was offered a brand-management job. "I told them I was in the wrong interview but they would not accept it and made me an offer," he says. "I refused, but they flew an executive over and convinced me."

> **'I did him a favour, which, as it turned out, has more than worked to my advantage.'**

At Procter & Gamble he discovered people could get trapped in old ideas. "I have a knack for being able to judge what marketing consumers will respond to," he says. "The competition has been slow to react, and it has taken them six years to stop saying 'Oh my!' about us and to do something. Having the idea is easy. Getting the guts to go out and do it is the hard part. The key is to keep things simple and not to get overcomplicated."

Butler still savours the moment that launched his business. "I bumped into Commissar some years later and told him he was the reason I shook up this business," he says. "I've never seen anyone go so white."

If you believe in yourself, it pays to advertise

**Original interview
9 March 1997**

Henry Lewis, the tycoon who founded Action Computer Supplies, began by begging for work in a newspaper.

Begging for work by placing an advertisement in the classified section of a newspaper may seem the last throw of a desperate man. But for Henry Lewis it yielded the break he needed — a decent job that eventually helped him form five businesses and become a millionaire.

An affable man, Lewis has an opinion about everything and has jumped from job to job. He has risen from humble beginnings in Cricklewood, northwest London, where he was educated at Mora Road secondary school. His father was a lorry driver and his mother a factory cook.

The only thing Lewis inherited from his parents was self-confidence, but today he lives in a plush flat overlooking a garden square in Earls Court and is founder-chairman of Action Computer Supplies (ACS), Britain's top mail-order supplier of everything to do with computers.

Floated in July 1996, ACS is valued at £93m, its shares having risen from 70p to 195p. At the age of 21, Lewis qualified as an engineer at the Electrical Research Association, but he saw that his boss earned little more than he did — despite having a degree from Imperial College — and decided to get out. So he placed a small advertisement in the London Evening Standard that read: "Electronics engineer requires design, development work. Anything legal considered".

Lewis got one reply. Edward Ling, a Chinese businessman based in London, asked him to work on a contract he was pursuing to install a monitoring system in jet engines. Ling won the contract at Bristol Siddeley and Lewis had a job. "I don't know if he employed me for my initiative or because he thought I was cheap and keen," says Lewis. "Either way, I was suddenly responsible for critically-important systems and had an amazing amount of responsibility. It brought the best out of me and over four years I developed opinions that would mould my values for my business career.

"I learnt the merit of being analytical. I was building early digital systems. They were the precursors to the computer but they were the size of wardrobes. The key is that nothing is impossible. I broke things down to basics and kept plugging away until I found a solution. I've never lacked self-confidence, which is scary when you don't have any talent."

Lewis was not happy being a conventional manager climbing the career ladder, reckoning his progress would be slow. "To take up a job solely as a career move is misguided," he says. "People put themselves in a secondary position, casting themselves as apprentices who always need to learn a little bit more before they become valuable. This way they always rely on someone else's help to get the job done.

The best way to develop a career is to take responsibility, and have the self-esteem to be always on one's mettle, pushing to do more."

It was a formula that did not always work. He was fired from what became Lintronics for being too cocky and took a further five jobs before he finally struck out on his own. "I suffered from a large dose of self-esteem," he says. "There was tension with Ling, we fell out, and I realised that ultimately I did not want to work for other people."

His next job was at Associated Electrical Industries. "I was told I had the gift of the gab and an outgoing personality," says Lewis. "My colleagues said I should combine my personality with my technical knowledge to sell computers, so I left and worked my way up to sales director of Electronics Associates. When my boss moved to Memorex, he took me with him."

Lewis became managing director in 1973 after a year in California. In 1976, however, he decided to set up on his own. He began with Computercall, backed by his brother. It offers a 24-hour service to computer users who need help and acts as an answering service for more than 100 computer companies.

Lewis then set up X-data, a computer equipment wholesaler. Launched with £55,000 of capital, it was sold three years later for £960,000. He also formed Multicomputer and Wall Data Europe, and in 1981 he set up his best venture, ACS, which started selling printer ribbons by mail order, gradually increasing its range.

Sales were £250m in 1997, accounting for 15% of the market. Lewis wants to

> **'Electronics engineer requires design, development work. Anything legal considered.'**

expand across Europe, having found that the key to success is finding a good niche and recognising your limitations. "Knowing what you are good at is not the answer," he says. "Knowing what you are bad at is the key. How many businesses fail at what they are good at?"

Name: **Henry Lewis**

Date of Birth
28 January 1939

Nationality
British

Present Company
Action Computer Supplies

Age when first in business
21

Education
**State Primary/Secondary then
Technical College**

Early entrepreneurial ventures
—

School holiday job
Small engineering workshop

Qualifications
Electronic engineer

First job
**Apprentice at Electrical Research
Association**

Sales/Profit before tax 1997
Sales: £250m Profit: £7.1m

Weeks holiday per year
Five weeks

Hobbies/Sports/Interests
**Golf; family of 6 children and
6 grandchildren**

Idiosyncrasies, eg, car owned
—

Power Of Persuasion

Peter Stringfellow
nightclubs

Jane Cavanagh
computer games

Ken McCulloch
hotels and restaurants

Gifi Fields
fashion

Paul Smith
fashion

Church put Stringfellow on right path

Original interview
26 January 1997

Peter Stringfellow's clubs offer topless dancers but he broke into business with help from a vicar.

The path to celebrity for Peter Stringfellow was unconventional to say the least. A Sheffield steelworker's son, Stringfellow survived a prison sentence, bankruptcy and two divorces to see his name in lights outside nightclubs on both sides of the Atlantic.

Stringfellow loves to shock — his latest enterprise is rolling out topless-dancing cabaret across the country — so no one should be surpised when he cites a vicar as the person who gave him his first break. "Vicar Jerome gave me my first break," says Stringfellow. "He let me rent St Aidan's church hall in Sheffield to stage live musical acts. I was 21 and just out of prison so he was a bit cautious, but he'd been an officer in the army, so he wasn't one of your wishy-washy vicars. He gave me a chance."

Stringfellow only needed one chance. He started making money on the third event and was soon earning five times his weekly wage. He decided to jack in his day job to make a living out of the gigs. He booked The Beatles, the Hollies and Screaming Lord Sutch.

"The Beatles changed everything," he says. "It gave me the first sight of the unlimited potential of business. I made a fortune. It was special to be part of that magic.

"Vicar Jerome was no fool; in many ways he was a bit of a wide boy. As soon as he saw me making money, he jacked up the rent. I learnt the hard way that you can't take anything for granted in business and you have to plan for the unexpected, even acts of God."

Hard work was no stranger to Stringfellow. As a boy his life revolved around paper rounds, a Saturday job delivering for the local bakery, which brought him all the broken pastry he could eat, and three nights a week as a projectionist at the local cinema, where he took a keen interest in the ice-cream girls.

"I came from an era where you had to work for your pocket money," he says. "It was never given. To have a job was all-important. Everyone worked." Stringfellow says in his recently published autobiography, *King of Clubs*, that he left school with no qualifications and had a series of jobs before starting his music business.

Date of Birth
—

Nationality
British

Present Company
**Stringfellow Restaurants
Ltd/Cabaret of Angels Ltd**

Age when first in business
21

Education
Sheffield Central Technical College

Early entrepreneurial ventures
**Selling firewood aged 12.
Organised a works coach party to
Blackpool in 1958**

School holiday job
**Van boy for bakery company
called Gillettes. Three nights a
week assistant projectionist at
local cinema**

Qualifications
None

First job
**Tie salesman, Austin Reed,
aged 15**

Sales/Profit before tax 1997
—

Weeks holiday per year
**In previous years two weeks, but
recently as many breaks as I want**

Hobbies/Sports/Interests
**None until 1997. I bought a
Sunseeker Superhawk 48 Boat**

Idiosyncrasies, eg, car owned
**Suzuki Jeep which is kept at the
berth with my boat in Majorca**

'**What makes a
difference is that
the staff know the
club is a part of me,
and that I am there,
hands-on,
every night.**'

He was a mechanic for half a day, an assistant barber, sailed around the world with the merchant navy, and came a cropper as a door-to-door salesman for Dobsons, a household-goods company.

He went to prison for three months for his part in selling 'liberated' stock. "I got on really well with the police-men and told them everything," he says. This is typical Stringfellow, who is down to earth with no apparent unpleasant side. The vicar may have helped him see the light in business but Stringfellow can rattle out ten other 'first' breaks — or watersheds, as he calls them — instrumental to his success.

The success of the church hall was followed by other larger venues until he mustered the capital to start Cinderellas and later Rockafellas in Leeds, eventually selling them to Mecca for £500,000. With that cash he opened the Millionaire Club in Manchester, which was sold to finance his entry into the West End. The Hippodrome and Stringfellows, the two West End nightclubs he founded, are both household names.

Later, Stringfellow tried to expand by branching out into America but he was hit hard by the recession. He was forced to close his clubs in Miami and Los Angeles but managed to hang on in New York by introducing topless 'table dancing', which turned the club into a success before he sold it.

In Britain, Stringfellow had to liqui-date the company that owned his clubs. The Hippodrome was sold to European Leisure for £7m but he quickly bought back Stringfellows nightclub from the receiver and it now forms the base of his business activities.

Stringfellow says he learns new skills continually: "My biggest lesson was in the recession. Failure was not some-thing I had ever tasted. I was fighting the whole American economy. I couldn't do anything. It was not a mat-ter of grabbing the microphone and working harder. I found it soul destroying."

Obsession and the will to succeed are what Stringfellow cites as essential entrepreneurial skills. In his case it may

> **'Vicar Jerome gave me my first break. He let me rent St Aidan's church hall.'**

also be a love of the limelight. Stringfellow's life revolves around his club. In fact he almost lives in it — his office and home are just two doors down the road. "What makes a differ-ence is that the staff know the club is a part of me, and that I am there, hands-on, every night. That's important," he says. "Celebrities like the fact that I'm there."

Switched on, the computer games queen

**Original interview
5 October 1997**

Jane Cavanagh founded her £20m business on the rights to six computer games salvaged from a liquidation by a French company.

As a child, Jane Cavanagh was more at home playing with circuit boards than dolls' houses. Her father had a small electronics business in Hardley in Hampshire, and she was fascinated with the gadgets he brought home.

She first showed entrepreneurial flair at 17. Cavanagh was desperate to raise funds to travel and hit on a way of making money by doing up cars. She went to a local auction and bought an MG Midget and a Fiat for £90 and spent half of her summer filing away rust and re-spraying the cars. She sold them for £300 and travelled on the profits for the rest of the summer. It was the combination of this resourcefulness and her early exposure to technology that enabled Cavanagh to spot the potential of the computer-games market.

Cavanagh left her job at BT to set up her own business, distributing computer games from Battersea, south London. Nine years later, her company, Sales Curve Interactive (SCI), is valued at almost £20m on AIM, and is a leading international developer of computer games. SCI, who employ 100 people at two sites, made a £1.4m profit on sales of £5.1m in 1997, boosted by the success of Carmageddon, a controversial driving game that came close to being banned — it gives points for the number of pedestrians knocked down. Cavanagh had not one break, but two. One gave her the spur to leave her job. The second almost sank her enterprise but turned out to be the making of the company.

The first break came while working for Telecom-Soft, a division of BT, developing its computer-game brands overseas. "I travelled to Japan and selected distributors and built up a portfolio of products ready for BT to sell down the telephone lines. About the same time games consoles were becoming phenomenally successful and I realised the industry had enormous growth potential, which I wanted to be part of."

Cavanagh took the revenue of her division from £40,000 to £420,000 in a year and began to make useful contacts. "I thought I could bring fresh ideas to an industry that was so young it had no defining parameters," she says. "It was always in the back of my mind that I'd start my own company and during my time in Japan it became obvious that this was the moment."

The opportunity came when Cavanagh was approached by one of her business contacts employed by FIL, a division of the French conglomerate, Thomson. The company wanted to expand its games development, and knew she was well connected in Japan. It offered her a position negotiating for the rights of arcade games for conversion into computer games. But Cavanagh had other ideas and wanted to start her own company. She convinced FIL to help her set up on her own, and persuaded it to give her £15,000 as a three-month advance.

She started SCI and from day one was in profit. Cavanagh's core business was brokering deals on behalf of FIL but she also employed programmers to transform the arcade games into computer format.

She did not own any of the lucrative licensing rights. "At the beginning, it was just me, the phone and Ben the dog," says Cavanagh. "Within six months, SCI had expanded to 10 staff but it was still very basic: each new employee was given a flat-pack desk and had to assemble it themselves."

But after eight months disaster struck when Thomson decided to wind up FIL. "It was our only client and owed us £20,000," says Cavanagh. There were six games that were only half finished and Japanese licences yet to be paid. Things looked unpleasant. "The Japanese do business on a culture of trust and I couldn't tell them we would not be able to keep our word."

Cavanagh went to Paris to see the French liquidator to explain the position but found he spoke little English. On her third trip he began to realise how personally important this was to her, and agreed to give her the deposits for the Japanese licences, and the rights to the six games in progress.

"This was a turning point. The games were 60% complete and were of little use to anyone else. It was like having half a painting — it is only worth anything if the artist that started it completes it. Overnight our business was transformed from being an agent for other people, to actually owning intel-

> **'I thought I could bring fresh ideas to an industry that was so young it had no defining parameters.'**

lectual property rights we could exploit." This she did, and SCI finished and distributed the games, which brought in profits of £50,000 in the first year and saved the company.

SCI now develops and publishes its own games, which are sold in 60 markets. Cavanagh says the key to starting your own company is finding the right product at the right time. "Choosing an industry that is going to grow is also important, and being naturally optimistic but realistic helps. I am also very tenacious and stubborn, which can irritate people but professionally it has its advantages."

Date of Birth
4 May 1957

Nationality
English

Present Company
SCI Entertainment Group Plc

Age when first in business
Own business at 30

Education
**Totton 6th Form College,
Hampshire; Southampton Institute**

Early entrepreneurial ventures
—

School holiday job
**Various — at 15 selling ice-creams
in local shop then at 18 a tour
guide in Paris**

Qualifications
Business Studies degree

First job
—

Sales/Profit before tax 1997
**(To June 1997) Sales: £5.1m
(To June 1997) Profit: £1.4m**

Weeks holiday per year
Five weeks

Hobbies/Sports/Interests
Riding, skiing, walking, holidays

Idiosyncrasies, eg, car owned
—

**'I am very tenacious
and stubborn, which
can irritate people
but professionally it
has its advantages.'**

Basement bargain led to hotel chain

Original interview
21 June 1998

Opening a bar in Glasgow that didn't sell spirits was a gamble that has grown into the £60m Malmaison chain for Scottish entrepreneur Ken McCulloch.

Using other people's money, or OPM, is a classic way to get a business started. That at least was the way Ken McCulloch, founder of the Malmaison hotel chain, got started. McCulloch's break came at 21 when he persuaded a hotelier to let him open Glasgow's first wine bar in the basement. A Glasgow bar that did not sell spirits might not in 1970 have seemed a great idea but it worked and within two years he had three outlets.

From bars he moved into hotels, opening up One Devonshire Gardens in Glasgow's smart West End district. A five-star "boutique hotel", it won Egon Ronay's Hotel of the Year award in 1994 and gave him the confidence to launch the Malmaison chain with backing from Robert Breare's Arcadian International group. Just how successful his concept was became clear recently when America's Patriot group paid £92m for Arcadian, a deal that valued Malmaison at £60m.

McCulloch, who lives with his family in Monte Carlo, is staying as Malmaison's chief executive and is masterminding expansion. He has come a long way since he started working life plucking chickens in a British Rail hotel. His father was a showbusiness reporter and impresario and his mother a Billy Cotton Band Show singer, and McCulloch was taken to many glamorous destinations as a child. Not surprisingly, with his entertainment background, he dreamt of being a rock star during his days at Gresham House, a Motherwell public school. But in the end he chose the hospitality sector. "The two professions are not dissimilar," he says. "You need to get it right out front, and you only get one chance. The show must go on."

From British Rail, he became a Stakis management trainee but at 21 he decided to strike out on his own. He says: "I wanted to start Glasgow's first wine bar — imagine setting up something that did not sell spirits in Glasgow. Yet I thought I could do things differently." McCulloch had no business experience and could not borrow for his plan. But he persuaded Harry Taylor, who had just bought Beacons hotel, to help him open La

Date of Birth
7 November 1948

Nationality
British

Present Company
**One Devonshire Gardens;
Malmaison**

Age when first in business
21

Education
Gresham House, Scotland

Early entrepreneurial ventures
**La Bonne Auberge, Charlie Parkers,
Spaghetti Factory, Rogano,
The Buttery**

School holiday job
—

Qualifications
—

First job
**Management Trainee, British
Transport Hotels**

Sales/Profit before tax 1997
—

Weeks holiday per year
—

Hobbies/Sports/Interests
**Football, motor racing, food, wine
and cigars**

Idiosyncrasies, eg, car owned
**Serious Porsche enthusiast;
Member of the International
Cigar Clan**

'You have to earn
your stripes, then
you have to have
total belief in your
judgement and your
ability to deliver.'

Bonne Auberge. Taylor took a risk but the rewards flowed in. The bar became a roaring success and gave its founder the confidence to expand. He says: "I just had to do something on my own that was really me. I had this blind faith that it would work, a total belief in myself."

His second venture was Charlie Parker's. By the time he launched it others were opening wine bars so he decided to move into cocktails to stay ahead of the pack, renting a 10,000 sq ft site in Glasgow's Royal Exchange Square. Half the capital came from bank and brewery loans, the rest from cashflow, and once again he had a winner. "It was a sensation and took off like a rocket," he says. Next he started the Spaghetti Factory, a restaurant, and a Charlie Parker's in Edinburgh. Initially it was not successful but he refined the formula and sold his business for £500,000 in 1981.

He took a year off but then opened Smiths, a piano bar, and teamed up with John McKenzie, a brewery executive, to relaunch Rogano, a restaurant founded in 1876, and The Buttery. One Devonshire Gardens started off with eight luxury bedrooms but was not big enough to make profits so McCulloch got £150,000 from 3i to buy three neighbouring houses, enabling him to take up the number of bedrooms to 27.

The idea for Malmaison came from a visit to America where he saw the success of high-quality, low-price hotels. The key was to find unusual but cheap sites, such as derelict churches, that could be developed at low cost.

After failing to get venture capital, McCulloch persuaded Breare that Arcadian could develop Malmaison and in 1994 the first two hotels opened in Glasgow and Edinburgh. There are now two more in Newcastle and Manchester where Mick Hucknall, of the pop group Simply Red, was an original investor. More hotels are planned for Leeds, London, Paris, and key European cities before the group turn their attentions to the States.

McCulloch succeeded, he thinks, because he took no notice of sceptics. "Everything is a hunch," he says. "But you have to earn your stripes, then you

> **'You need to get it right out front, and you only get one chance.'**

have to have total belief in your judgement and your ability to deliver. Sometimes within the corporate sector you have to stop making sense. But hang on to your beliefs, never dilute a good idea."

Fashion guru hid guilty secret under his flares

**Original interview
18 January 1998**

A fractured knee gave Coppernob's Gifi Fields his big break when a buyer took pity, thinking he was disabled.

Making people feel sorry for you can be the secret to getting a business off the ground — or so Gifi Fields discovered. Fields, who started Coppernob, the women's fashion label, in 1976, accidentally created his first break.

He managed to convince a woman buyer at Harrods to stock his clothing range after she mistakenly thought he was disabled. The break took his business up a rung, from the trendy market stall where he cut his teeth to the big time as an international clothing designer. It came at the end of the 1960s, when Fields, then aged 19, converted his mother's washing machine into a dye-tub and started a small cottage industry with his friends making and selling shirts and trousers. "The Sixties were great and people could not get enough of my shirts."

After a year he had two small shops on Kensington High Street and London's King's Road but aspired to bigger things. He secured an interview with Liz Treisman, a womenswear buyer at Harrods' trendy Way In department.

She said the department was not opening up new accounts but humoured him because he was persistent. The weekend before the meeting, Fields went riding near Canterbury in Kent, but as he was taking a fence the horse in front kicked backwards and caught his knee, breaking it. Fields's leg was put in plaster from the ankle to the thigh, and since flares were all the fashion at the time, he was able to get his trousers over the cast, effectively hiding it. "There was no way I was going to miss my first appointment at Harrods, so I hobbled in ready to schlep all my garments around, and the girls made a tremendous fuss to help me. I had my leg out horizontally and when Treisman walked into the room. She said, 'No, no, don't get up,' and had a cursory look at what I had to offer, almost immediately making an order for some tartan knickerbockers." This was the break Fields needed to raise his profile. "It was the start of a relationship," he says. The following week Treisman called to ask for more garments because his order had sold out. A few weeks after, she called him back to see some more of his range.

"My plaster had come off and I was

walking normally when I returned to Harrods. Everyone was staring at me as if I had three heads. Treisman saw me bend my leg, and said, 'You must be the luckiest man alive. I'm not supposed to be opening up new accounts, but I felt sorry for you. I didn't think you had a leg, I thought it was wooden'." This misunderstanding got his foot in the door, and led to other opportunities at Harvey Nichols, Selfridges and then Bloomingdale's in New York, and Galeries Lafayette in Paris.

In August 1974, after cashflow problems, Fields sold the business, which was called Rag Freak, to Associated Services London, and signed a seven-year design contract. But after 18 months he left.

He had built a reputation as a rising star and at 23 he had also picked up some basic business skills. In 1975 he teamed up with a manufacturer, Tony Chrysostomou, who put up some cash while Fields designed and sold the garments. They founded Coppernob, and in the first four months it made £26,000 profit on sales of £200,000. Fields bought Chrysostomou out for £180,000 in 1979 when he was employing 12 people. By 1983 Coppernob was making a profit of £500,000 and he bought Snob, a retail chain with 13 outlets, as a means to sell his garments. Four years later Fields sold Snob to Etam for £4m after building the chain up to 28 shops.

At one point he controlled a 6.5% share of the womenswear market. He still heads Coppernob and designs and manufactures women's clothing, making garments for River Island, Sears,

and Great Universal Stores. In 1997 Coppernob had 32 employees, and made £161,000 on sales of £12.2m.

Fields was born in California, but moved to Shrewsbury, Shropshire, with his mother when he was 11. He later earned pocket money working in a fishmonger's in London's Golders Green. "I made a fortune in tips as all the Jewish women loved my ginger hair and Californian service." Fields, who is the brother of the late Randolph Fields, the airline entrepreneur, first discovered his talent for making clothes when he was kicked out of home for refusing to go to university.

> **'There was no way I was going to miss my first appointment at Harrods.'**

Whilst travelling in Morocco, he saw some fabric he liked and got a girlfriend to make shirts from it. His friends loved them.

Fields says he has succeeded by being more interested in invention than profit. "Great products speak for themselves," he says. "Most good entrepreneurs learn more from their mistakes than through their successes. Trial and error is everything. It is something you cannot learn at university."

Date of Birth
29 June 1951

Nationality
American

Present Company
Coppernob

Age when first in business
19

Education
William Ellis School, Shrewsbury

Early entrepreneurial ventures
**Trotsky International Rag Freak,
1970-71**

School holiday job
—

Qualifications
**Fellow Chartered Institute of
Marketing**

First job
**Selling lemonade and sweets in
Los Angeles, aged 8**

Sales/Profit before tax 1997
Sales: £12.2m Profit: £161,000

Weeks holiday per year
Four weeks

Hobbies/Sports/Interests
**All sports, theatre, reading and
writing both fiction and non-
fiction, all music, food and wine,
current affairs and politics**

Idiosyncrasies, eg, car owned
Vibrant red curly hair

'Most good
entrepreneurs learn
more from their
mistakes than
through their
successes. Trial and
error is everything.'

Back room boy cut out for World Cup glory

Original interview
14 June 1998

Paul Smith learnt his trade while helping a friend launch Birdcage, a Nottingham clothing shop. He realised he wanted his own firm but did not have enough money to get started.

His break came when another friend gave him floor space in a shop at no cost — and thus was born the Paul Smith label. He now owns a global brand selling in more than 40 countries. Profits in 1997 were £6.5m on sales of £171m and Smith was in the news around the time of the World Cup for designing the bespoke beige suits worn by the England football squad.

The son of a credit-draper, he went to Beeston Fields Secondary School in Nottingham and failed every exam. At 15 he took a menial clothing warehouse job and dreamt of being a professional racing cyclist. But that dream ended when he broke his leg and he then started to focus on clothing.

Smith educated himself about his trade at Birdcage — he helped find its site, he painted it, learnt how to dress its windows and to source clothes from manufacturers. After four years he decided to go out on his own and was encouraged in this by his Royal College of Arts trained girlfriend, Pauline Denyer, who liked his ideas and energy, and became his designer.

He began by trying to accumulate launch capital, supplementing his income for two years by working as a consultant to London shops, and organising clothes production by liaising with factories. By 1970 he had £600 but it was not enough to open a shop and he needed help.

During his breaks at Birdcage he met Douglas Hill, a tailor, and had chatted about his dreams and frustrations. In the end this paid off. "I kept telling him I could be a success and one day he just said, 'Take my back room, just have it, and stop talking about it', and that was the start of Paul Smith."

Hill's back room was 12ft square and could be reached only through a narrow corridor. Smith painted the passageway green, much to the horror of neighbours, and installed spotlights. He then knocked down a disused door that overlooked the street and put in a pane of glass to transform it into a shop window. "The key was individuality. It was a rebellious time but all the stores were selling more or less the same thing and it was hard to buy interesting

Name: **Paul Smith**

Date of Birth
5 July 1946

Nationality
British

Present Company
Paul Smith

Age when first in business
21

Education
Beeston Fields Secondary School

Early entrepreneurial ventures
**Making ties on my mum's sewing
machine in the front rooms**

School holiday job
Petrol station attendant

Qualifications
—

First job
**I worked on Broadway aged 15.
I was a gofer in a clothes
warehouse in Nottingham**

Sales/Profit before tax 1997
Sales: £171m Profit: £6.5m

Weeks holiday per year
—

Hobbies/Sports/Interests
**Cycling, swimming,
photography**

Idiosyncrasies, eg, car owned
1956 Bristol 405 (Liver Red)

'The key has been to explore alternative routes that no one else has thought of.'

clothes outside a few cities. Success came through selling the right style of clothes — no compromise."

Smith did not pay rent for three months, and then only 50p a week. People liked his 'more interesting' designs but his finances were precarious and it made economic sense to open the shop only on Fridays and Saturdays. Pauline, who is still his girlfriend after 30 years, was responsible for most of the early designs. Eventually the shop started to motor as word spread about the clothes and customers travelled from other cities such as Leeds and Manchester.

Smith still needed to supplement his income by doing consulting work for other shops but was able in 1976 to shift to opening six days a week. He then began to expand, borrowing £3,000 from Hill and a few hundred from his father to launch a wholesale label. In 1977 he moved to a London bedsit and began selling clothes to buyers from Bloomingdales and Seibu of Japan.

By that time people saw him as a trendy new designer. This gave him the confidence to look for a London shop and he hit upon Covent Garden, which at that time was not the shopping destination it is now. After looking through the letterbox of 44 Floral Street, a derelict building, he made an offer to its owner, a retired baker. Smith had no money and raised £15,000 from a bank and a clothing manufacturer, but that did not come close to the £35,000 asking price.

"I told the baker I could not raise the

£35,000 and had only managed £25,000. We had built up quite a rapport and he said I could have it for the £25,000. But then I was forced to tell him that I had told a fib and really only had £15,000. This was too much to expect him to knock off the price. But he seemed to like me and had no family and he offered to lend me the remaining £10,000, which I paid off each month."

The money from selling clothes wholesale was set aside to spend on renovating the shop. Finally fit to open in 1979, it became a hit — a year later it employed 15 people and had made a

> **'I kept telling him I could be a success and one day he just said "Take my back room".'**

£16,000 profit on sales of £309,000.

In 1982 Smith bought the shop next door and opened an outlet in Japan. Eventually the brand was sufficiently strong in the Far East for Smith to license the Paul Smith name and today he is a cult figure in Japan where more than 200 shops sell £140m of goods.

Smith says success comes from enthusiasm and energy. "I love life and people and have never gone down any obvious routes," he says. "The key has been to explore alternative routes that no one else has thought of."

Raising The stakes

David Pearl
property development

Richard Koch
venture capitalism

Sir Tom Farmer
car tyre retailing

Karan Bilimoria
alcoholic beverages

Mike Taylor
printing

Laura Tenison
fashion

Arnold Clark
car dealerships

Date turned into hot property

**Original interview
10 May 1998**

The love of an older woman, together with an interest-free loan, laid the foundation of David Pearl's £100m property empire.

Mixing business with pleasure can lead to trouble, but for David Pearl it served as his first break and transformed his estate agency into a property investment company. Structadene, his company, owns more than 1,000 residential and commercial properties around Britain valued at £100m. In 1997 it made £5m profit on sales of £15m and now employs 22 people.

He began his career after leaving school at 15 and spending four years packing cardigans into boxes. He switched to property on the advice of an estate agent friend called Norman Silver. After two days' work, Pearl decided he liked the business and set about starting a firm with Silver in 1965. "I always wanted to become really wealthy, and having come from a very poor background gave me the will to succeed. I remember visiting my Auntie Lillie's flat in Regents Park, and seeing fitted carpets in every room in the house, and hot running water. I knew that was for me; it acted as an early incentive."

Silver's father lent the pair £100 to start up Pearl & Coutts. "Silver and Pearl would have sounded like a firm of Jewish moneylenders," says Pearl. "Coutts sounded as though we had been around for years and gave it some sort of respectability." After five years letting flats and factories from an office in Hackney, east London, the two split up. Silver wanted to set up in the West End and Pearl was not interested. It did not take him long to realise the real money was being made in owning property, rather than managing it for others. He changed the name of the business to Structadene, but it was difficult to get on the property ladder.

His first break came in 1971 when a woman wanting to sell her house came into his office. "She took a shine to me. She was quite a bit older and we talked about how I would raise the cash to buy her house and I took her to dinner. She knew my ambitions and after we had spent some time together one thing led to another and she wanted to help me. After a few months of seeing her, she showed her gratitude by selling me her house with what was effectively a 100% interest-free mortgage. I paid it off over five years at £8 a week, and rented it out at £12 a go. It would have been difficult

Date of Birth
25 October 1945

Nationality
British

Present Company
Structadene

Age when first in business
19

Education
**Secondary Modern, Crowland
Road, left aged 15**

Early entrepreneurial ventures
Setting up estate agency

School holiday job
**Cutting grass for neighbours and
delivering fruit and veg for local
greengrocer**

Qualifications
—

First job
Packing cardigans into boxes

Sales/Profit before tax 1997
Sales: £15m Profit: £5m

Weeks holiday per year
**One or two. He does not like
holidays**

Hobbies/Sports/Interests
Property, swimming

Idiosyncrasies, eg, car owned
Owns 15 mountain bikes

**'The key has been
building up a
rapport, making
decisions fast,
and being a man
of my word.'**

to get a foot on the housing ladder but she really gave me the leg-up I needed."

Starting with that one property, Pearl set out to establish a portfolio. He began by buying another house for £3,000, borrowing the cash from a firm of moneylenders. But he took a risk. The firm wanted collateral, and Pearl gave it the deeds to his parents' home. He continued buying properties for some years, and by 1978 had a portfolio of 50 buildings, but he says he had no idea how to run a business and did not produce a set of accounts until 1979 when he brought his former banker into the business as financial director.

"Once I had the freedom of working for myself it was the most wonderful feeling. I worked the hours I liked and when a pretty girl came into the office I could shut up shop and take her out for lunch."

Pearl wound down the property-management side to his business and concentrated on buying homes and offices, often at auction. He was able to buy bundles of properties cheaply and re-sell some of them at much higher prices. Sometimes, during the rampant property boom in the early 1970s, he would double his money in days. His second break came in 1980 and it took his business into a different league.

He heard the Jesus Hospital Estate in Bethnal Green, an estate of 260 run-down artisans' cottages, was up for sale. The manager was trying to buy it and told the trustees it was worth £800,000. Pearl put in a £1.2m offer, knowing it was worth more. "I bought the development but didn't have the money to complete the deal, and didn't even have enough for the deposit. I sweated, and ran off to find someone to lend me the money."

He found a backer in Joseph Schonfeld, for whom he had managed property, and with whom he had a good relationship. Schonfeld saw it was a bargain. The deal tripled the size of his property portfolio overnight, and brought in an instant income because the homes already had tenants. He still owns a third of the houses after buying out Schonfeld some years later. They now sell for around £200,000 each.

> **'Once I had the freedom of working for myself it was the most wonderful feeling.'**

He has since made further, much larger, acquisitions of commercial property, particularly in London's West End, some with joint-venture partners. He survived the recession of the early 1990s, not least by trimming his costs to the bone.

He says he owes his success to being streetwise. "That's the best education," he says. "I don't need to know about balance sheets. I don't know how to read one. I know what's going on inside my head. I had no responsibilities and took chances I would never take today. The key has been building up a rapport, making decisions fast, and being a man of my word."

LEK man's success was on the cards

Original interview
21 September 1997

Richard Koch reckons his talent as an entrepreneur comes from gambling skills picked up at Oxford.

Richard Koch first realised he had a talent for making money when he gambled his student grant on the 2.30 at Ascot and raised enough to fund his living expenses for the whole term.

As a student reading history at Wadham College, Oxford, he became bored with mundane vacation jobs, finding betting shops and poker more profitable. He claims to have made a few thousand pounds each year on gambling, and says the skills he learnt outside his tutorials helped him to become a successful entrepreneur.

He uses the same criteria in deciding whether to back a horse as he does when choosing the companies in which he invests. He made his first million by the time he was 30 through trading in shares while working for Bain & Co, the management consultant. That gave him the confidence to quit (with two colleagues) to set up his own business, the LEK partnership, which was making profits of £10m after six years. Koch puts much of his success down to his gambling and feels

it enabled him to accept the risk of leaving a well-paid job.

At Bain he had become a partner within a year but after three he was getting bored. "I was super-successful and everything pointed to me staying for years, but I had always wanted to have my own business, and had been toying with the idea for some time. All I would have to do was persuade the clients that I could add value. It was a matter of finding the right time to leave the business."

Koch wanted to set up his own company with two colleagues, Iain Evans and Jim Lawrence, but discovered they had travelled to Bain's Boston head office to put the idea to Bill Bain. Koch was desperate to be involved and found their telephones permanently engaged when they returned. He cycled from his flat in Bayswater, west London, to Evans's house in Kew to find they were setting up a new consultancy but Bain was threatening legal action to stop it.

"They started the firm and I joined them when the lawyers gave their blessing with an investment of £250,000 each, and won the legal battle. I looked after the strategy side and

137

focused on consulting, acquisitions and gathering information. In our first year we made a £500,000 profit and each year after that doubled in size, profits and staff. It was magic and my best business experience."

But he got bored again and left the consultancy after six years to set up his own venture-capital company, Strategy Ventures, with £4m raised from the sale of his 23% LEK stake. After 18 months searching for the right opportunity he read that Filofax was in trouble. To save it he invested £1m with Robin Field, his partner, and then created a new strategy for the company. The shares rose from 15p to 210p, the price paid by Day Runner, an American rival, in 1988.

Koch was also the original backer of Belgo, the London restaurant chain known for Belgian beer, mussels and frites. Here a £350,000 investment turned into around £5m. Koch has also invested progressively a total of around £2.5m into MSI, a British hotel group that has six three-star outlets and net assets in 1988 of £20m. Koch now lives part of the time in South Africa, where he works as a venture capitalist.

Koch reckons the disciplines he learnt from his gambling days have been the key to equipping him to start his own business. "Business is about timing — knowing what to do and when to do it," he says. "The similarities between a game of poker and making an investment are obvious; everything hinges on absolute confidence and a high degree of probability.

"In business it is essential to find out the one thing you know that others don't and back it heavily. The one legacy my father gave me was to gamble — we used to go to the races, and play cards — I began to enjoy playing for money." Koch discovered poker at Oxford but could never remember all the rules. He had to be reminded at each game and this led his opponents to mistake him for a novice. "What you have to do is persuade people that you are reckless and can't play and look slightly drunk," he says. "Then, when you have a good hand and the stakes are high, you nip in there and make a killing." Koch found it prudent

> **'All I would have to do was persuade the clients that I could add value.'**

to use this technique sparingly to survive at Oxford and quickly learnt that there was no such thing as a sure bet.

He hated his first job at a Shell oil refinery. His independent and insubordinate approach did not go down well and he was marked down as having limited potential. He then worked for a year for a pet food company owned by Mars, before deciding that paid employment was not for him. "I saw my American MBA and consulting as a launch-pad for regaining my independence. Now I avoid the distraction of working for other people. I'm a bad employee and need to build my own castles in the air."

'Now I avoid the distraction of working for other people. I'm a bad employee and need to build my own castles in the air.'

Name: **Richard Koch**

Date of Birth
28 July 1950

Nationality
British

Present Company
None (self-employed)

Age when first in business
21

Education
BA & MA (Oxon), Wadham College, Oxford. MBA with distinction, Wharton Business School, Philadelphia

Early entrepreneurial ventures
Selling stamps on approval, aged 13

School holiday job
Refuse collector

Qualifications
MA, MBA

First job
Personnel Assistant, Shell International Petroleum Co

Sales/Profit before tax 1997
—

Weeks holiday per year
About ten weeks

Hobbies/Sports/Interests
Tennis, cycling, badminton, running, horse-racing, visual arts, ideas, writing

Idiosyncrasies, eg, car owned
Written 11 books, the most recent being *The Third Revolution* published by Capstone Publishing. Owns sports cars, but hates taxis and always travels by tube and bus in London (except when cycling). No interest in spending money. Current net worth around £20m

Failure put Kwik-Fit on road to success

**Original interview
13 April 1997**

When a bonus for selling tyres failed to materialise, Sir Tom Farmer decided to set up his own business.

Sir Tom Farmer is made like a classic car: finely tuned, a king of the road. And he is seen in Scotland as a bit of a local hero. But a classic motor is still just an old car, and Farmer steers a well-worn course.

He is founder-chairman of Kwik-Fit, the exhaust, tyre and brake company. Founded in 1971 as a one-stop shop in Edinburgh, it has grown to a £418m public company with more than 1,800 outlets.

He is a devout Catholic who makes an annual pilgrimage to Lourdes and has built a reputation as a highly focused, steely-eyed wheeler-dealer who has risen from nothing.

He believes people work for two things: enjoyment and the wage packet. Farmer was prompted to start out in business by a combination of money and bad news.

Just turned 23, he was selling tyres from a van in east Scotland. When he did not get the bonus owed to him for the third time he left his job and decided to go it alone. "I was driving back through Edinburgh when I saw an empty shop in a good location and thought it would make a good tyre shop," says Farmer. "I had little money or experience and had to convince Mr White, the factor (landlord), who worked on behalf of Edinburgh University, that I could meet the £5-a-week rent and be a sound tenant."

He has proved that without doubt: he took home £3.45m in 1996, has a private jet, a KBE, and his own island. "Eventually I managed to convince White with my enthusiasm and energy that I was a good salesman and I begged, borrowed and improvised so that I could set up Tyres and Accessory Supplies and start selling discounted tyres on sale or return," says Farmer.

The business took off after a newspaper article highlighted small firms, including his own, that were challenging manufacturers by offering cheap tyres. The following day there were 40 cars outside his shop.

Farmer was the youngest of seven children, raised in a two-bedroom tenement flat in Leith. The son of a shipping agent, he was schooled at Holy Cross Academy. He earned spending

Date of Birth
—

Nationality
Scottish

Present Company
Kwik-Fit

Age when first in business
16

Education
Leith

Early entrepreneurial ventures
Rebuilt bicycles, cleaned cookers

School holiday job
As above

Qualifications
—

First job
Selling tyres

Sales/Profit before tax 1997
Turnover: £472m Profit: £55m

Weeks holiday per year
**Various, depending on
circumstances**

Hobbies/Sports/Interests
**Kwik-Fit people, Kwik-Fit
customers. Many charities
supported**

Idiosyncrasies, eg, car owned
**Much in demand as a public
speaker**

'The lesson I learnt was in perception. The more I failed the more successes I had.'

money by doing a paper-round and working in a chemist shop.

He started Kookers Kleaned when he was 15, going from house to house cleaning ovens. The Kwik-Fit name shows an equal disregard for spelling. "Creating an identity that is unique and easy to remember is important," says Farmer.

He left school shortly after and joined a tyre firm as a stores boy — as soon as he learnt how to drive he collected used tyres for a remould factory and was paid commission.

His colleagues used to collect one load and come back and sort out the paperwork. Farmer did as many collections as he could during daylight hours, saving the paperwork for evenings and weekends.

He launched Tyres and Accessory Supplies in 1964, and soon had a small chain, selling out four years later to Albany Tyre Services for £450,000. He remained a director for two years and then, aged 30, retired and moved to San Francisco. But boredom prompted him to return to Scotland and, inspired by the American 'muffler' shops, he started Kwik-Fit, selling out once more for £750,000.

The purchaser, GA Robinson, was a public company and gave Farmer a seat on the board. Within months it ran into difficulties during the 1974 three-day week and Farmer responded by taking control, selling off its loss-making businesses, buying out other directors' shareholdings and renaming the group Kwik-Fit.

By 1980 Kwik-Fit had grown to 50 shops and it has since expanded through acquisition and organic growth. It now has 1,800 outlets and has diversified into insurance.

It reported profits of £43.3m in 1996, 19% up on the previous year, and is planning to break into new foreign markets.

Farmer says he is in business to make profits and is not ashamed of that. "Value for money is what matters," he says. "It has become an obsession to look after the customer. My job is not to manage Kwik-Fit but to lead it.

> **'Creating an identity that is unique and easy to remember is important.'**

"The point is the difference between delegation and abdication, and experience counts for a lot. The biggest problem this country has is learning there is no shame in failure." Farmer learnt early if someone wanted to be successful he had to accept failure along the way. As a young salesman he discovered that every five calls he made resulted in only one order. "But the lesson I learnt was in perception," he says. "The more I failed the more successes I had."

Cobra man's charmed life

**Original interview
7 June 1998**

Indian beer importer Karan Bilimoria raised his start-up capital by bringing in polo sticks from his own country after the Falklands war halted supplies from Argentina.

A contract to sell polo sticks to Harrods was the start of Karan Bilimoria's serious business career. Today Bilimoria heads Cobra Beer, owner of Britain's biggest bottled 'Indian' beer.

The Falklands war gave him his opportunity. Supplies of Argentinian polo sticks halted as a result of the British embargo and Bilimoria, the Cambridge-educated son of the then head of the Indian Army, filled the gap through contacts his small import–export operation had with his home country. Bilimoria had captained the Cambridge polo team so he knew the market.

He and his partner, Arjun Reddy, could also show the Indian sticks' advantages: they were bamboo, not willow, and thus lighter, but the clincher was that they were half the price of the Argentinian sticks. Along with the polo sticks he subsisted on his meagre earnings from trading in embroidered jackets and fabrics, and at the time of his polo move he was £20,000 in debt. So to get started he had to borrow £290 from his partner to buy a battered Citroën 2CV, in which he would transport the sticks.

It was hardly a gigantic business but it did generate sufficient capital for Bilimoria's move into beer. "I started at Harrods, which initially refused to deal with me because I had not formed a limited company. As soon as I had, I returned to the deputy buyer who was still not interested, but I was persistent in the knowledge that his supplies from Argentina had been hit hard by trade restrictions."

Harrods eventually placed an order for 200 sticks. This gave him credibility, and other stores followed suit. "We had the advantage of having a foot in both camps, India and England, and asked ourselves where Indian companies fell down. The answer was that they did not market themselves well over here and we went out to find Indian companies we could represent, and started importing products."

He spotted that Indian beer could be a lucrative niche market after an experience in an Indian restaurant. English

143

friends would typically ask him to order but they were not very happy when he ordered the only brand of Indian beer available in Britain at that time.

"I used to eat in Indian restaurants a lot and friends would get me to order, but the beer was not like home. The only decent beer was Kingfisher until one day they started brewing it under licence in Britain and it tasted completely different," he says.

"It set me thinking there was a niche, Indian restaurants being so popular, and I should do something myself."

His first thought was to import Pals beer, brewed by Mysore Breweries and the main brand in the Indian army's officers' messes during his childhood.

But it did not travel well and sharing the name with a dog-food brand did not help sell it in Britain. So he visited Mysore and worked with its head brewer to create a new beer, which he named Cobra.

Mysore's only available bottles were 660ml — far bigger than the typical beer bottle — but Bilimoria used this to differentiate his product. "It was a real disadvantage, which I turned into a unique selling point, convincing restaurateurs that these were what people drank in India. I sold them restaurant to restaurant from the back of my 2CV."

By 1995 Cobra had branched out from Britain into exporting to Belgium, France, Italy and the Netherlands. As a result, Bilimoria was able to sell a quarter of the shares to friends to raise £500,000 and the following year Cobra was being brewed in Britain.

In 1998 the company, which sells to retailers including Marks & Spencer, Tesco and Fortnum & Mason, made profits of £77,000 on sales of £4.25m and has ambitions to quadruple turnover by 2001.

Bilimoria comes from a privileged background. He was educated at Lushington, the prestigious English boarding school in Ooty, a hill station in southern India. He then took a university commerce degree in Hyderabad, went to England to qualify as a chartered accountant with Arthur Young's, and then read law at Sidney

> **'It set me thinking there was a niche, Indian restaurants being so popular.'**

Sussex College, Cambridge, where he funded his studies by working his holidays auditing accounts for Gerald Ronson, among others.

"It was a real eye-opener," he says, "and whetted my appetite for starting my own business. Nothing should stop you if you have the will to succeed."

Date of Birth
26 November 1961

Nationality
Born in Hyderabad, India. British resident

Present Company
Cobra Beer Ltd

Age when first in business
27

Education
'O' Levels at Lushington Hall, Ooty, India

Early entrepreneurial ventures
Selling polo sticks, fashion accessories, fabric/interior design material, beer

School holiday job
Newspaper deliveries

Qualification
B Com (Hons), MA (Law), ACA, Business Growth Programme 1998, Cranfield University

First job
Part-time bookkeeper while at accountancy college, then trainee chartered accountant, Arthur Young, City, London

Sales/Profit before tax 1997
(To July 1998) Sales: £4.25m Profit: £77,000

Weeks holiday per year
Varies, but work a few hours per day keeping in touch with the office when abroad

Hobbies/Sports/Interests
Polo, golf, swimming, current affairs, scuba diving, tennis, squash

Idiosyncrasies, eg, car owned
Perfectionist. Loves food, particularly Indian. Favourite dish, biryani and parsee dhansak. Loves beer, real ales and top premium lagers

'Nothing should stop you if you have the will to succeed.'

Bank gave printer the chance to print money

Original interview
2 November 1997

Mike Taylor, chief executive of Fulmar, got his firm off the ground when a new bank manager saw his potential.

The most critical relationship aspiring entrepreneurs have is usually with their bank managers. This was an early lesson for Mike Taylor, chief executive of Fulmar, the printing company, valued on the stock market at £30m.

Taylor's first break came when he persuaded Bill Dimond, a young manager at National Westminster Bank, to lend him the £5,000 he needed to start his own business. The results paid off for both sides: Taylor has since built a business that reported profits of £5m on sales of £39m in 1997, while Dimond was eventually put in charge of starting a new-business centre for NatWest in Richmond, Surrey.

Taylor started Croydon-based Fulmar with one printing machine in 1972 and was profitable from day one. In 1980 he moved to his first purpose-built factory, which employed 12 people and had sales of £1.3m. In 1996 he floated the company, which currently employs 450, and at the start of 1997 he bought Royle Group, the greetings-card company, for £1.5m.

On starting Fulmar, he borrowed £4,000 from his father but it was not enough — everything hinged on Dimond, who was new to NatWest's Hounslow West branch. He agreed to give Taylor the loan. Taylor kept Dimond as his bank manager, following him to four different branches, until Dimond retired in 1997. "Banking is all about relationships and I felt it important to stay with someone who knew our business and the industry. He has been through two deep recessions with us during the past 25 years and the relationship has proved to be extremely valuable and key to the success of Fulmar."

As a child, Taylor always wanted to be involved in the printing business. His father was a director of a printing firm in Liverpool and the young Taylor fell in love with the world of ink and hot-metal printing. "I was exposed to it at an early age. I was just eight when dad took me round the factory and made me a lead slug with my name spelt backwards on the old hot-metal press. I kept it for years."

When Taylor left school he joined Bayer, the drug company, as a print buyer, and while he was working for

Date of Birth
13 July 1947

Nationality
British

Present Company
Fulmar Plc

Age when first in business
24

Education
Thames Valley Grammar, 5 'O' levels; London College of Printing, 4 'O' levels, ONC & HNC Business Studies, City & Guilds

Early entrepreneurial ventures
None

School holiday job
None. I went fishing

Qualifications
See above

First job
Management Trainee, Printing Co

Sales/Profit before tax 1997
Sales: £39m Profit: £5m

Weeks holiday per year
Five weeks

Hobbies/Sports/Interests
Sailing, motor racing, Koi carp

Idiosyncrasies, eg, car owned
Personal car, Ferrari 355 Spyder. Raced cars for 14 years in UK and Europe culminating in British Sports 2000 champion in 1987. Entering the Arc in 1999 to race from the Canaries to St Lucia

'You have to work harder than you ever imagined and be totally committed.'

the multinational he realised he hated working for other people. "I was the tiniest cog in a wheel and found it difficult to work where you don't do things your way," he says.

But one particular late-night incident acted as the spur that prompted him to leave. "It had gone ten o'clock. I was doing the work of two people when the chairman's assistant came round to lock up. She came across me still working there." When asked what he was doing, Taylor explained he was doing the work of a former colleague who had left the company and had not been replaced. He wrongly thought his efforts had finally been noticed and would count in his favour. Instead he was called into his manager's office and told that he was obviously not efficient or organised enough to do the job in normal hours, and had to pull up his socks. He was furious and set about making plans to leave.

"I remember it as clearly as if it was yesterday. That sort of keenness should be encouraged and not trampled on," he says. "It was a defining moment and I decided I wasn't going to work for people who think a job well done is a job done between nine and five."

Taylor's career as an owner-manager did not have a smooth start. The first banker he approached refused to lend him the cash he needed to launch. "The manager had been at NatWest for years, he was very old and set in his ways and refused me point blank," he says. But he did give Taylor one good piece of advice. "He told me he was due to retire in a month and a younger

manager was coming along who might be prepared to take the risk," he says. "His advice made all the difference — I didn't care which one of them gave me the loan so long as I got it."

Fulmar was soon trading well, thanks to a lot of hard work. Taylor started it in an old pickle factory where he rented part of the first floor. There was no lift, so when paper was delivered Taylor would stack it in a dumb waiter and crank it up by hand. He would operate the press, answer the phone, and make deliveries himself. His mother, who did the books, was his first worker. "My wife would bring fish and chips and sit with me until the

> **'I felt it important to stay with someone who knew our business and the industry.'**

early hours of the morning. I was the cheapest printer in London with tiny overheads. Within three months I employed a machine minder, and I had a second printing press within nine. The business just took off from there."

The key to being a successful entrepreneur, says Taylor, is being prepared to sacrifice everything. "The company comes first," he says. "You have to work harder than you ever imagined and be totally committed. It is easy to say 'Sod it' and walk away when the bank is on your back. It is virtually you against the world and you have to go out to get it."

French cottages gave birth to babywear firm

**Original interview
8 February 1998**

Laura Tenison's holiday-home venture gave her the money to launch JoJo Maman Bébé.

Raising the money to launch a new enterprise is often the first hurdle entrepreneurs have to overcome. For Laura Tenison it was a hurdle she almost didn't clear.

Tenison, founder of JoJo Maman Bébé, a maternity and babywear manufacturer and retailer, had a childhood ambition to get into the clothing business. But days traipsing around banks looking for money got her nowhere. Eventually her luck changed when she discovered that she might find her seedcorn capital for JoJo Maman Bébé through property dealing.

Tenison's break came in the early 1990s when buying homes in France was all the rage. It came more by accident than design. As a fluent French speaker, she agreed to travel to Brittany with a friend, Kate Edwards, who was looking to buy a house.

"We met up with a fat French estate agent who was drunk. We put him in the back of the car and drove around to different properties but he fell asleep and began to reek of garlic. The incident made me realise there was a real opportunity for someone to do a decent job linking British househunters to decent properties, and there was no reason why it could not be me. I just had to tap what I saw as a niche in the market. I called the company Aquilla."

She made her real money by finding derelict cottages for buyers and then organising their renovation. Once the gites were renovated she took charge of letting them for her clients. She built the business up over three years, dividing her time between France and England.

Tenison showed good timing in taking her profits. At just 24, she sold the business for £70,000 a few days before Black Monday and was then in a position to follow her dream.

"I finally had the cash to start my clothing business," she says. On returning to Britain she did some market research to find a niche in clothing. Demographics showed there was a baby boom and a gap in the market for maternity wear.

"Just because women become pregnant it doesn't mean they suddenly do not want to look good. I moved into a small unit in Lots Road, Chelsea,

149

southwest London, and decided to make a collection of clothes as nice as any in the high street but tailor them to fit pregnant women."

Tenison did the design and sourced fabrics but contracted the manufacturing to small units in Britain, Europe, and South America. She established a warehouse in Pontypool, Wales, close to where she grew up and her first worker was her former nanny.

In her first year Tenison produced two catalogues and advertised in mother and baby magazines. She turned over £67,000 and broke even in the second year, winning the British Telecom retailer of the year award in 1993.

She now employs 16 people and made a profit of £70,000 in 1997 on sales of £1.1m. She plans to open shops in north and south London — where many of her mail order clients live. She is also expanding her range.

Tenison was determined to have her own clothing business as a child. It all started when she was nine and her teacher taught her how to make soft toys for children in Africa.

She was more interested in making clothes for the dolls and soon she was sufficiently skilled to auction them in the playground. At 12 she was bought a sewing machine by her mother and she spent much of her spare time making clothes.

Tenison studied French and Italian at technical college in Cambridge, and continued as she had as a child to spend most of her evenings making clothes though now she found a market for her work through her friends. Her mother tried to make her do the Season, but she was a reluctant debutante, and would turn up to parties with her diplomat father's old briefcase full of samples. Tenison says: "I took commissions from these ghastly people and found it much easier to sell to men."

After college, she took a job with Aquascutum where she picked up basic retailing and selling skills, and decided to leave to raise money to start her own business.

'Demographics showed there was a baby boom and a gap in the market for maternity wear.'

Tenison says her success stems from hard work and perseverance. "You have to be prepared to forgo everything for the business," she says. "Until I had my son I would much rather work than do anything else. Enthusiasm is what counts."

'You have to be prepared to forgo everything for the business. Enthusiasm is what counts.'

Name: Laura Tenison

Date of Birth
1 September 1966

Nationality
British

Present Company
Jojo Maman Bébé Ltd

Age when first in business
**Small businesses since childhood.
First full-time business, aged 23**

Education
**Monmouth School for girls, 8 'O'
levels; Queens College, Harley
Street, London, 2 'A' levels**

Early entrepreneurial ventures
**Making and selling clothes at
school**

School holiday job
**Waitress/bar work plus making
and selling clothing**

Qualifications
Very few

First job
**Dunn & Bradstreet — copy chasing
for French and Italian advertising**

Sales/Profit before tax 1997
Sales: £1.1m Profit: £70,000

Weeks holiday per year
**Between two to four weeks.
Depends on business. Most
holidays tagged on to
business trips**

Hobbies/Sports/Interests
**Lots, but no time to do them.
Travel, skiing, cycling, trekking,
house renovation**

Idiosyncrasies, eg, car owned
**MG convertible and Mercedes
estate, but always cycle
when possible**

Car dealer hit road to top with travelling bar

**Original interview
16 March 1997**

Arnold Clark made money to start his career by running a bar for dances.

Arnold Clark does not like to admit his first break had no connection with cars. He is Scotland's top car dealer, the face fronting advertisements for his Arnold Clark company, and, according to the 1997 Sunday Times Rich List, Britain's 130th richest man.

He feels his customers will be disappointed to learn his first break came when he was running staff dances for companies in Glasgow's public halls. He has since built a motor group with 72 showrooms and sales of £700m, according to 1997 figures. This puts Clark's company among Britain's top 10 dealers and makes it Scotland's biggest, with a 15% share of the Scottish market.

Clark's original opportunity came through Robert Sutherland, a publican and family friend. Sutherland allowed Clark to use his drinks licence to organise dances and functions in the late 1940s.

This helped him to save enough money to break into the car business. Sutherland also taught Clark bookkeeping, customer values, hard work and discipline.

At 21, Clark left the Royal Air Force, where he had been a car mechanic and instructor. He wanted to work with cars, but lacked the experience to manage a garage, yet was overqualified as a mechanic.

"I had no job and was petrified," says Clark. "I was technically skilled and determined to get into the car business, but needed to get work to earn some money. None of the masonic halls had drinks licences, so Sutherland let me use his and I organised staff dances with my travelling bar.

"Sutherland was more my mentor than a boss, teaching me the basics of business, and I taught myself management skills through the employment of casual labour. I never talk about this as I think of motoring as having been my only profession; since I was 17 this was the only four years I was away from it." Clark's perseverance paid off. In 1953 he had saved enough to start trading cars.

Clark grew up in Glasgow, where his father was a steel worker and his mother worked for a butcher. He was called

Date of Birth
27 November 1927

Nationality
British

Present Company
Arnold Clark Automobiles Ltd

Age when first in business
22

Education
To 5th Year Isle of Arran (during the war); RAF Weeton Technical School Instructor, Motor Mechanics

Early entrepreneurial ventures
Milk run; evening paper deliveries

School holiday job
Farming

Qualifications
FIMI (Fellow of Institute Motor Industry)

First job
SCWS apprentice shoe design, aged 14 (1 year only)

Sales/Profit before tax 1997
£20m

Weeks holiday per year
Not many

Hobbies/Sports/Interests
Art — own collection. Sailing, comp racing now retired

Idiosyncrasies, eg, car owned
Simply love cars. Drive Alpha Romeo 156 V6

'In French, entrepreneur simply means businessman, nothing more. That's all I think I am.'

up for military service at 17 and afterwards spent four years with the travelling bar before selling his first car. His early success came from his rapport with customers. "It was about building a good name, a sound business, and being polite and honest," he says.

"One of my biggest breaks came with the Suez crisis, which should have been my downfall. Petrol was rationed and I saw this as an opportunity. I travelled up to Wick in northern Scotland and bought cars on the cheap because demand was low due to petrol shortages and I sold them for full value in Glasgow where petrol was not so short. I made enough money to open my first showroom."

In 1959 Clark opened his first new-car dealership. By 1963 he had five branches, offering top makes such as Daimler and Jaguar. Then he diversified into breakdown recovery, repairs, hire cars, a driving school and insurance. Sales doubled in the past six years, and 1997 figures show a rise in profits to £20m.

Clark exploits his reputation as the 'grandaddy' of Scottish car retailing in his adverts. But he only started to think about strategy after sales hit £20m. At that point he knew his company needed a direction.

"I'm an opportunist — I have never actively sought anything," says Clark. "I have always expanded during recessionary periods, being approached by receivers selling dealerships at reasonable prices after they had fallen.

"I've always been canny and kept within the ambit of my resources. I have had no strategy or budgets, just plenty of cash. I stick to routines and do not allow myself to diversify. I'm a creature of habit."

His only regret is no longer having executive cars in his portfolio. He thinks some manufacturers consider his business too mass-market. Clark does not plan to float on the stock market and is grooming some of his nine children to take over from him. They are, no doubt, learning about what Clark thinks is the key to his success.

> **'I'm an opportunist — I never actively sought anything. I have always expanded during recessions.'**

"It is dedication, hard work and having super managers. What I started in the 1950s and 1960s is different from what I do today. The structures for getting on are much easier these days," he says. "I've always lived by the premise that when you drive towards a corner, you turn round it rather than through it. I don't believe people are born as entrepreneurs. In French, entrepreneur simply means businessman, nothing more. That's all I think I am."

07 988 756 882

07 988 756 682